Nordic Modernism

Scandinavian Architecture 1890–2015

Nordic Modernism

Scandinavian Architecture 1890–2015

WILLIAM C. MILLER

Foreword by Juhani Pallasmaa

THE CROWOOD PRESS

First published in 2016 by
The Crowood Press Ltd
Ramsbury, Marlborough
Wiltshire SN8 2HR

www.crowood.com

British Library Cataloguing-in-Publication Data
A catalogue record for this book is available from the British Library.

ISBN 978 1 78500 236 6

To Beverly and her valiant struggle with Alzheimer's disease

Typeset by Servis Filmsetting Ltd, Stockport, Cheshire
Printed and bound in India by Replika Press Pvt

Contents

The Image of the North

THE NORTH IS SIMULTANEOUSLY A MYTHI-cal and concrete notion, mythical in a mental, symbolic and historical perspective and concrete in terms of being one of the most stable and balanced corners of the world and an ideal of well-functioning modern democracies. The North has traditionally been seen as the remotest region of Europe with a rather disadvantageous climate. However, the current warming of the global climate and the eventual opening of new northern shipping routes, as well as the newly found natural resources in the Arctic Ocean, are potentially changing the peripheral location of the area. The notion of 'The Northern Dimension' reflects this new attention and has already become part of today's political and economic terminology. The current environmental and cultural developments may well alter the dialectics of centre and periphery. In today's world of forceful technologies, we tend to forget the fact that it is due to natural conditions, the Gulf Stream, that human culture at the level of the Nordic countries, located largely north of the 60th latitude, has been possible in the first place.

As a mythical mental image, the North is not a place, but rather an orientation, an atmosphere and a state of mind. Historically, 'the North' has referred to the unknown. Virgil, the Roman poet of the Augustan era, used the term Ultima Thule, the ultimate north, as a symbolic reference to an unknown far-off place, a non-place and even an unattainable goal. This mythical echo still reverberates in the dreams and thoughts of Southern cultures. The Southern cultures have traditionally dreamt of the North, whereas the Nordic people and artists have longed for the South, particularly the Mediterranean world. Characteristically, due to the idealized imagery of Southern deciduous forests and cultural landscapes, Finnish artists did not paint their dominant coniferous or mixed forest before the mid-nineteenth century. Something of the ageless mythical feeling of the North still exists even in the minds of today's Swedes, Norwegians and Finns, whose countries extend well beyond the Polar Circle; northern Lapland and the Arctic Ocean continue to project an air of danger, mystique and the unknown.

The concepts of the Nordic countries as well as of Nordic architecture are products of the modern era, as they did not exist in a wider international consciousness before the late nineteenth century. The monarchies of Sweden, Denmark and Norway have long and varying histories, whereas the idea of national independence emerged in Finland only towards the end of the nineteenth century and was decisively promoted and formulated by the arts. Alvar Aalto makes the point that only through the Finnish Pavilion at the Paris World Fair in 1900 did Finnish culture enter an international consciousness and dialogue.

For the first time, Finland appeared on the continent with tangible materialized forms as a source of culture that might influence others, rather than simply being on the receiving end … It is difficult for a small country to make its psyche understood in a global context, the more so if it has a language that is, and will remain, alien to the otherwise close-knit family of European languages … We need a language that has no need to be translated. One might say that the existence of a new language was gradually revealed in Paris in the spring of the year 1900.[1]

Here Aalto refers to the material language of architecture and the non-verbal language of music. This view of the significance of Eliel Saarinen's Finnish Pavilion applies to Nordic architecture altogether; since the late nineteenth century, the Nordic countries have had masterful individual architects who have become part of the world history of this art form. Not to underestimate the contributions of Nordic writers, artists, composers and scientists for the Nordic identity, I venture to argue that it is through the modern democratic societies and general cultural achievements in the material arts, such as architecture, that the Nordic countries are known in the larger world today.

The Interplay of the Material and the Mental

The Nordic countries[2] are often seen as a unity and indeed, the cultures, lifestyles, values and artistic expressions of the four countries (Iceland, the fifth Nordic country, is not included in this book) are similar and their long intertwined histories have tied these nations together in a multitude of ways. But the differences are equally noticeable. The differences are distinct in the geographies, landscapes, human temperaments and cultural habits, as well as artistic sensibilities. Generally we are not very sensitive to understanding differences in the material world, but the differences are as clear as between cultural behaviours and languages. We habitually underestimate interactions of environments and culture, settings of life and human character. Yet our environments of life and our minds constitute an indivisible continuum. As the visionary American anthropologist Edward T. Hall argues:

The most pervasive and important assumption, a cornerstone in the edifice of Western thought, is one that lies hidden from our consciousness and has to do with a person's relationship to his or her environment, Quite simply, the Western view is that human processes, particularly behaviours, are independent of environmental controls and influence … The environment provides a setting which elicits standard behaviours according to binding but as yet unverbalized rules which are more compelling and more uniform than such individual variable as personality … Far from being passive, environment actually enters into a transaction with humans.[3]

We still underestimate the interactions of environments and culture, settings of life and human character and do not see or acknowledge their interdependencies. Yet, as the American literary scholar Robert Pogue Harrison suggests poetically: 'In the fusion of place and soul, the soul is as much a container of place as place is a container of soul; both are susceptible to the same forces of destruction …'[4] The common view that architecture is an individual artistic expression of the architect is simply false, as architecture is necessarily a consequence of countless historical, geographic, social, cultural and economic factors. The essence of the artistic expression is hardly purely individualistic either. 'We come to see not the work of art, but the world according to the work', Maurice Merleau-Ponty argues wisely, and this view certainly applies to architecture, too.[5]

Towards Modernity

Due to their 600 years of shared political history and rather similar geographic conditions, Sweden and Finland share more similarities, perhaps, than the other Nordic countries, although they also share their complexly intertwined histories. Even language conditions our ways of perceiving the world and dealing with it conceptually, intellectually and emotionally.

Consequently, it is reasonable to argue that our mother tongue is our first domicile. As a Ural-Altaic language, Finnish is fundamentally different from the other Nordic languages, which belong to the Indo-European language group. The fact that Finland has a 6 per cent minority population, mainly located on the south and west coasts, who speak Swedish, further complicates the interplay of similarities and differences. In any case, the differences are equally clear as the similarities. Due to her location, Denmark has naturally been more connected with continental European cultures and its general mentality is more urban and perhaps more sociable and open-minded. Historically, the Norwegians have been somewhat isolated due to their rugged mountainous geography and deep fjords and this condition has been reflected in their character, as well as their cultural products.

The art of architecture has developed firmly in the Nordic world without major conflicts, all the way from the late nineteenth century until today. Even the peasant and small town urban vernacular traditions were assimilated in the emerging modernity. The Nordic Classicism of the 1920s, sometimes called 'Light Classicism' because of its casual and good-humoured tone, drew its inspiration from the *architettura minore*, the urban vernacular of northern Italy, and blended it with the indigenous Northern building traditions. This restrained but elegant classical language paved the way for modernity; most of the leading exponents of Nordic Classicism turned into modernists within a year or two. The new architecture, which emerged in the end of the 1920s and was usually called 'Functionalism' (the terms 'Rationalism', 'New Realism' and 'New Objectivity' were also used), soon adopted softer regional and traditional features and turned into the unquestioned and unchallenged architectural expression of the progressive modern Nordic societies. Instead of orthodox stylistic attitudes, Nordic architecture in general has had an assimilative character. It is exceptional on a global scale in that modernity became the culturally accepted style early on and historicist or revisionist aspirations have not re-emerged since.

Even the postmodern and deconstructivist trends of the 1980s had only a minor influence in the North. The modernist formal language, both in architecture and the design of everyday objects, became a constitutive ingredient in the identities of modern Nordic societies. The movement of '*Vakrare vardagsvara*'[6] (more beautiful everyday objects) arose in Sweden in the 1920s and turned into an unchallenged cultural condition in all the Nordic countries.

Architecture and Nordic Identities

The socio-economic and political history of Sweden and the ideals of social justice and equality have been reflected especially in Swedish architecture. During the entire era of modernity, Swedish architecture, and especially housing, has been guided by a strong social and sociological orientation, as well as the ideals of solidarity and the modern state as 'the People's Home'. Artistically, this social orientation of Swedish architecture has sometimes seemed to turn into an architectural weakness and lack of artistic autonomy, because of a patronizing attitude. However, in retrospect, it is evident that the acceptance of the requirements for domesticity has been a form of responsible social empathy as opposed to an architect-centred formalist aestheticization. The domestic bliss depicted in the delightful paintings of Carl Larsson reveals this mental inclination towards cosiness and domestic bliss, which can be felt in much of Swedish architecture even today.

Danish architecture is traditionally a product of a sense of urbanity and higher social compactness. The flat, cultivated landscape has also been imprinted in the Danish character, settlements and architecture. The intimate scale, refined materiality and detailing, as well as craft skills, speak of established human relationships, urban professionalism and lively traditions of trade. Danish architecture also reflects a tradition of human forbearance and enjoyment of life in comparison with the sense of seriousness of Finnish and Norwegian buildings. A distinct lightness and elegance have characterized the Danish architectural tradition.

In accordance with the relative isolation and harshness of life, Finnish architecture has always reflected individuality, but even more importantly, the prevailing forest condition. Certain features of Finnish architecture, such as its sense of tactility, the frequency of irregular rhythms and appreciation of natural materials, evidently echo the forest condition, which nowadays is more often a mental and experiential attitude than an actual condition. We could here speak of a 'forest mentality' as the guiding reference for spaces and forms. For a Finn, since the ancient times, forest has signified safety, protection and comfort, as opposed to Central European cultures for which forest usually implies threat and discomfort. In the olden days Finnish life meant living in communion with the forest. Forest was the peasants' entire world; it was there that they cleared land for farming and caught game and from the forest they took the raw materials for their buildings and implements. The forest was also the sphere of the imagination, peopled by characters of fairytale, fable, myth and superstition. The forest was the subconscious realm of the mind, in which feelings of safety and comfort, as well as fear and danger, lay. 'We Northerners, especially the Finns, are very prone to "forest dreaming", for which we have had ample opportunities up to now', even Alvar Aalto, the cosmopolitan, once said.[7] In Finnish culture, a modesty or restraint, 'the noble poverty' of peasant life, can still be detected as a common value.

Until recently, Norwegian architecture has reflected a strong consciousness of tradition and the rugged mountainous landscape and sense of isolation can be detected in the character of Norwegian architecture. Seafaring traditions have likewise had their impact on Norwegian life, architecture and crafts. During the past decades, however, architecture has changed in Norway, perhaps faster and by a greater amount in its general character than in the neighbouring countries, towards the dominant international architectural language. As a consequence,

the traditional ground cannot be identified in today's Norwegian buildings as clearly as just a couple of decades ago. The recent national wealth from oil resources has dramatically changed the economic conditions of the country, but the newly acquired wealth hardly shows in daily life, which speaks of a maturity of the collective values.

The Societal Role of Architecture

Architecture is undoubtedly the most collective of art forms and it takes place at the intersection of tradition and innovation, individuality and collectivity, convention and uniqueness. It is also bound to balance between aspirations for differentiation and assimilation and the Nordic temperament has rarely wished to stand out from the group or context. As a consequence of their gradual evolution, Nordic architectures have become rooted in these social realities more strongly than in other parts of the world and they have had a determined societal mission. In post-war Finland, for instance, architecture decidedly aspired to raise the self-consciousness and esteem of the people, shattered by the disasters of the war. Rapid reconstruction and high aesthetic quality became a form of mental recovery and a source of pride. The fact that in 1998 Finland's Council of State approved 'The Finnish Architectural Policy' – presumably the first governmental architecture policy in the world – underlines the special role that the art of building has been given in Finnish society. In the entire North, architecture has been used as a means of societal reaffirmation and unification rather than of differentiation and polarization. In the early 1950s, Alvar Aalto saw the task of public buildings as setting a model of architectural quality for the construction of settings even for daily life and work.

The emerging 'class-free' society is still more vulnerable than the bourgeois society generated by the French Revolution, for it includes larger numbers of people, whose physical well-being, sense of citizenship and cultural awareness will depend critically on the correct ordering of the institutions and areas serving the public.[8]

The cultural, ethnic and social homogeneity of the Nordic nations, as well as their long period of undisrupted social and economic development, have reinforced this attitude of solidarity. However, the abrupt increase of differences in income levels in today's neo-liberal consumer society threatens this traditional sense of societal coherence, togetherness and equality as well as the Nordic ideal of the welfare state. The current unrest in Europe and the largely uncontrolled mass immigration of refugees poses an unexpected challenge for the Nordic social balance, but also for individual judgement and sense of responsibility.

Light and Silence

We tend to think of regions and places primarily in terms of geography, landscape and material settings, but often the most important single quality that creates the sense of a unique place is the ambience of light. In his book *Nightlands: Nordic Building*, the Norwegian architectural historian and theorist Christian Norberg-Schulz emphasizes the power of the natural illumination in the North: 'It is precisely light that defines the Nordic worlds and it fuses all things with mood … In the North we occupy a world of moods, of shifting nuances of never-resting forces, even when light is withdrawn and filtered through an overcast sky.'[9] No doubt the character and dynamics of light are tangible; the night-less summer as well as the day-less winter, when light seems to radiate from below, as snow picks up the slightest source of light from the firmament and reflects it back, are special conditions of Northern illumination. Even sunrises and sunsets, as well as cloud formations, rain and snowfall, have atmospheres of their own that are distinctly different from any other location on earth. As a consequence of this ever-changing dynamic of light,

Nordic architecture is more sensitive to light than architecture elsewhere. Architects of the Northern countries, more than in other regions of the world, design special light fixtures for their buildings in order to articulate even artificial light. Light is a precious gift for the dweller of the North and it is naturally celebrated in life and architecture. Although historical buildings often contain beautiful arrangements of light too, the understanding of the expressive potential of illumination seems to be a modern sensibility.

Twenty years ago I had the opportunity of seeing an exhibition of Nordic painting of the turn of the nineteenth and twentieth centuries titled 'The Northern Light' at the Reina Sofia Museum in Madrid. The paintings were hung thematically, irrespective of their country of origin and I was struck by the uniformity of feeling that the paintings were steeped in; scenes of lonely human figures in landscapes, dim dusk and twilight, a sensation of humility and silence and a distinct sense of melancholy. Indeed, the sense of Nordic melancholia was unexpected and striking. This unified nature of Nordic sensibility for illumination was revealed by the sharpness of the Southern light as much as the silence was accentuated by the urban bustle of the Spanish streets. I had not understood the unity of the Nordic condition quite so clearly before this simultaneous encounter of the Northern and Southern light. No doubt we tend to become blind to our own environment and everyday reality and we recognize them only when valorized by opposite conditions.

The North and the Consumerist World

During the past two or three decades, the Nordic countries have regrettably lost some of their unique and exemplary qualities as architecture increasingly reflects global values and fashions. At the same time, the strong subconscious connections between the built surroundings and patterns of life have also weakened. During the past three decades,

Spain has become the most inspired and inspiring country in the field of architecture. Why that should be the case is not easy to explain. Perhaps the liberation from a long period of political suppression has released creative energies, whereas the Nordic countries have taken their societies and economic and cultural achievements too much for granted or as self-evident conditions. Creativity never arises from self-satisfaction and complacency. Consumerist habits and values have also weakened the idealist quality of Nordic modernity, as the tendency for societal idealization has often been replaced by individualistic aestheticization. The Nordic countries may be losing some of their identity and character through accepting processes of internationalization and globalization too uncritically. On the other hand, the general values in architectural judgement around the world have favoured a spectacular and visual imagery and Nordic architecture has not offered many examples to be celebrated by this misguided orientation. So the sensationalist ambience of the international architectural publications may somewhat explain the relative absence of the Nordic countries from the international scene of celebrated architecture.

I do not believe that architects today should try to develop deliberately regionalist features using local vernacular or historical examples or thematized aspects of landscape and culture. Architecture is too deeply rooted in the collective mental ground and cultural past to be turned into consciously thematized or manipulated strategies. Simply knowing and respecting one's own identity and cultural heritage sensitizes one for the subtleties that support the experience of a specific place, culture and identity. Nordic post-war architecture projected an optimistic and modern egalitarian attitude, but echoed simultaneously a traditional sense of materiality, craft and scale and, especially, a touching humility and compassion. The most beautiful quality of Nordic tradition even today can well be its modesty and sense of realism and appropriateness, combined with a subtle aesthetic sensibility. 'Realism usually provides the strongest stimulus to my imagination,' Alvar Aalto confessed.[10]

Juhani Pallasmaa,
Architect SAFA, Hon. FAIA, Int. FRIBA
Professor Emeritus

ARCHITECTURE IS A MANIFESTATION OF human culture and society realized in a particular place or location. The importance of place or location cannot be underestimated as it directly impacts building, for nature plays her inextricable role in the making of human habitats. While society determines and defines our building types and their purpose and meaning – church, school, town hall or airport – the particular character of the natural world a building inhabits directly impacts its making. For nature determines experiential qualities like dark versus light, hot versus cold, rough versus smooth and humid versus arid, and natural phenomena like clouds and rain, forests, deserts, oceans and dust storms. At the same time nature provides the resources needed for human construction: wood, stone, metals, turf and soils and water. As such, the very different places we have chosen to live provide unique sets of resources to use in realizing architecture. It is humankind's capacity to produce meaningful, expressive spaces and places from those resources, thus releasing our cultural and creative energies.

'Scandinavia' and 'Nordic' are two terms often used interchangeably when discussing northern Europe. Traditionally, Scandinavia is considered a historical and cultural-linguistic region which included the kingdoms of Denmark, Norway and Sweden. Norway and Sweden are located on the Scandinavian Peninsula, while Denmark is situated on the Danish islands and Jutland. Taking a broader perspective, the term 'Nordic countries' includes Denmark, Norway and Sweden, along with Finland and Iceland and their autonomous regions – the Åland Islands, the Faroe Islands and Greenland. The connections between the Nordic countries have a long history and in the post-World War II period a common articulation of interests through the Nordic Council and Nordic Council of Ministers.

This discussion of modern and contemporary architecture will include Denmark, Finland, Norway and Sweden (Fig. 0.1). These four countries engaged interactively with each other and played important roles in the development of modern architecture and the modern welfare state. As such, the terms 'Scandinavian' and 'Nordic' will be used interchangeably, as well as another common reference, 'the North'. All three terms reference and suggest a region with a particular physical and cultural character, identity and affiliation.

Often when looking at a world globe our view is with the equator at eye level; the poles recede from our view. But viewing the world from the North Pole provides a very different perspective. It is a view defined by a particular series of natural phenomena: snow, ice, water, short dark winter days and the aurora borealis, long light-filled midsummer nights, an ever-changing cloudy sky and forests. The people of Scandinavia are united by inherited ties of culture, political experience and social sympathy. Moreover, their way of life is conditioned by the distinctive region which they inhabit at the north-western extremity of the great Eurasian land-mass; sea-bound, northerly and on the whole infertile (*see* Fig. 1.1).

Owing to its geographical position off the beaten track of Europe, Scandinavia did not find itself part of the great invasions which repeatedly swept across Europe after the fall of the Roman Empire. A great majority of the current inhabitants of Denmark,

Fig. 0.1 Map of Scandinavia showing the countries of Norway, Sweden, Finland and Denmark and their major cities. (Illustration: Freeworldmaps)

Norway and Sweden are descendants of the Vikings. The Finns are a different ethnic group, but have shared 2,000 years of history with their neighbours. And there are the Sami, a nomadic people of eastern European origin who live in Lapland, the northern part of the Scandinavian Peninsula. While the Nordic people, throughout history, have always been widely scattered and living in rural conditions, today the Scandinavian countries are some of the richest, most successful, urbane and progressive modern societies. The humanistic foundation of the welfare state has resulted in exceptionally high levels of education, universal health care and accessible social and cultural services distributed in an egalitarian manner.

My interest in Scandinavian architecture and Nordic modernism in particular, began as an undergraduate student in the School of Architecture and Allied Arts at the University of Oregon. The School had a faculty lecture series that during my time had

several faculty members who took sabbaticals in Scandinavia, and Finland in particular. They gave lectures on the then current Nordic architecture, often focusing on the architecture of Alvar Aalto who was building much in the 1960s. What struck me at that time, and still holds true, were the following characteristics of Nordic architecture: simplicity yet complexity in design and expression, strong response to the setting and a socially and functionally responsive architecture. During that period I had the opportunity to meet Alvar Aalto when he lectured at the Abbey in Mount Angel, Oregon and in my final year to engage in a special independent study of the Finnish master's work.

Several years later, entering the academic world from architectural practice, I found that one was expected to have a research or scholarly agenda to ensure success. It was at this time that Scandinavian architecture became my scholarly focus, beginning with the work of Aalto and Finnish architecture and then expanding to the rest of the Nordic countries. Over my teaching career a number of institutional and foundation grants and awards supported my research and its concomitant travel. I would like to thank the following institutions and foundations for their support over the past thirty-plus years: Kansas State University for three research grants; the College of Architecture, Planning and Design at KSU for a faculty development grant; the National Endowment of the Humanities for a 'Travels to Collection' grant; the American-Scandinavian Foundation for a research fellowship; the University of Utah Research Committee for two grants; and a grant from the University of Utah Teaching Committee. The resources supplied by these foundations and institutions supported my scholarly, publishing and lecturing endeavours, the development of courses on Scandinavian architecture and now the groundwork for this book.

During the course of my travels to the North, several individuals have been particularly helpful in developing my understanding of the unique qualities of Nordic architecture. I very much appreciate the insights provided me by Juhani Pallasmaa, Reima and Raili Pietilä, Göran Schildt, Elissa Aalto, Pekka Korvenmaa and Kristian Gullichsen. I would further like to thank Juhani Pallasmaa for writing such a thoughtful foreword to the book, as his insights are always illuminating, engaging and evocative. A special thanks to my former student Krysta Mae Dimick for allowing me to reproduce a number of her photographs as illustrations for the volume.

As a final consideration, experiencing architecture is a pilgrimage activity, as one cannot merely read about it. While this work examines the past century and a quarter of Nordic architecture, providing an overview and assessment of its characteristics and qualities, it is hoped that it will stimulate the reader to venture north and engage in discovering the unique experiential qualities of Scandinavian buildings within the context of their particular world; as Juhani Pallasmaa would suggest, to encounter the buildings in a direct and sensuous interaction for a more complete understanding of them and their place in the Nordic world.

Chapter 1

THE NORTH: LIFE ON THE EDGE OF THE WORLD

'NORTH' AND 'SOUTH' ARE FAMILIAR names defining geographical domains with specific character and identity. Travelling from the north to the south in Europe, one experiences the warmth of the sun-drenched classical landscape of the Mediterranean. In contrast, Scandinavia is a northern world: a world distinguished by a harsher climate with birch, fir and pine forests; fjords, lakes and rivers; glacier-etched valleys and granite outcroppings; and a sun set low in an ever-changing sky (Figs 0.1 and 1.1). In summer there is the never-setting midnight sun, while in

Fig. 1.1 The harsher Northern climate is illustrated in this aerial photograph of the winter snow covering Scandinavia and the frozen upper portion of the Gulf of Bothnia. (Photo: Image courtesy Jacques Descloitres, MODIS Land Rapid Response Team at NASA GSFC [Public domain], via Wikimedia Commons)

Fig. 1.2 Nedre Oscarshaug provides one of the best scenic vantage points along the National Tourist Route through the Sognefjellet Mountains in Norway. One of the route's arts projects, a glass telescope by architect Carl-Viggo Hølmebakk (1997), provides the names of the peaks and gives an overview of the surrounding Hurrungane massif. (Photo: Krysta Mae Dimick)

winter there is the aurora borealis animating the dark northern night.

What makes this world different: is it the light, the land itself, the vegetation, or the built environment which is somehow different? Indeed, it is all of these. In the North it is often overcast, rainy and grey and in such weather the materiality of things is emphasized, with moods being created (Figs 1.2 and 1.3). This seemingly inhospitable climate with its challenging topography hardened the population, producing a particular resolve. In the North, the necessity to establish direct and personal contact with one's surrounding environment is defined by the deep awareness that one is an integral part of nature. Here one is not a spectator but is engaged with nature, for nature impacts Nordic life, society and culture, as well as its architecture.

Scandinavian landscapes bear the powerful imprint of the last Ice Age, which ended some 10,000 years ago. For aeons northern Europe was completely covered with ice; when the earth's climate became warmer the ice gradually retreated northwards. Lakes and fjords filled the U-shaped valleys dug out by the mighty glaciers which once covered Scandinavia (*see* Fig. 7.16). Moraine deposits formed ridges such as the hills of southern Finland and the river valleys and enclosed lakes in other parts of Scandinavia. The Norwegian architect and architectural theorist Christian Norberg-Schulz, in his book *Genius Loci: Towards a Phenomenology of Architecture*, defines the Nordic forest as a romantic landscape characterized by numerous phenomena, with an 'indefinite multitude of different places'. It is a discontinuous ground surface that has a varied relief due to rocks, roots and depressions.[11]

Extreme variation of climate and sun has produced unique conditions of light throughout Scandinavia, making it a most precious commodity. The sun is relatively low and creates a varied play of light and shadow. It is a landscape that brings humankind back

Fig. 1.3 The forest, clouds and shimmering water on an undulating Finnish lake illustrate the notion of a space of moods and atmospheres within the Nordic landscape. (Photo: Author)

to a distant 'past'; a past experienced emotionally rather than understood as allegory or history. Water is often present as a dynamic element, be it sea, fjord, lake or river. Within this world we find that Northern space is primarily a clearing in the ubiquitous forest or an opening made by water. It is always a space of moods as the sky is continuously modified by clouds (Fig. 1.3).

Light informs us instantly that we are no longer in the South. Light provides the environment with its primary character in defining the Nordic world. Sunlight is the source of heat, illumination and well-being in a world that is often cold and dark. Scandinavia enjoys almost continuous daylight during the summer and is plunged into darkness during the winter. Even during the summer the intensity of the light remains weak when compared to the South, diluted by the low angles of incidence (*see* Figs 4.9 and 5.13). In the winter the light is almost horizontal with the sun barely peeking above the horizon. And the way

light percolates through the forest conditions the way Scandinavians see their world.

The Nordic attention to light overlies another quite opposite tradition: as much as any force, it is the brooding darkness of winter that also identifies the North. As Norberg-Schulz writes in *Nightlands: Nordic Building*: 'In the North it is only on winter nights that the sky becomes large, whole. Over the snow-covered earth, it vaults, saturated with a particular dark light.'[12] The blackness of the Nordic night is a place of wonder, containing its own subtle beauty of light and colour: a luminescent moon, dazzling stars and the aurora's colourful ethereal ripples. The silvery glow of the Nordic night is captured wonderfully in Harald Sohlberg's painting *Winter Night in Rondane* (1914) (Fig. 1.4).

While the Nordic countries are dissimilar in topography and vegetation, their skies share a subdued light that imbues the entire region with mystery. More than the landscape, it is the atmosphere that

Fig. 1.4 The silvery glow of the Northern night is captured in Harald Sohlberg's luminous *Winter Night in Rondane* (1914). (Photo: Harald Sohlberg [Public domain], via Wikimedia Commons. Located in the National Gallery, Oslo, Norway)

tells people they have reached the outermost rim of Europe. The Nordic sky is ever-changing as the weather rolls across the region; within a blue roof is the theatric energy and turbulence seen in the drifting clouds, the changing light patterns and whorls of mist.

From the tumbling streams cascading from the Norwegian glaciers filling the fjords with cold green water, to her rock-edged river valleys and the weaving of water and land in southern Sweden, to the shimmering blue waters of Finland's extensive lake district and the saltwater waterways defining Denmark's island environs, water is another critical element in providing mood in the Nordic world (*see* Fig. 1.3). For much of its history Scandinavia was rural and isolated and long-distance communication throughout the region was easier by water than by land. Therefore the seas, oceans, fjords, lakes and rivers were extremely important for development and commerce in the region and to access other lands. It is no accident that the capitals of the Nordic countries are located on water, as are her other major cities and towns (*see* Figs 1.5, 6.11 and 7.9).

Capturing Northern Moods and Atmospheres: Scandinavian Landscape Painting

The Nordic world is a world of moods and atmospheres, as witnessed through experiencing the forests with their irregular ground plane, under the ever-changing sky, with extremes of light and dark and the varied water qualities: this notion is captured by Scandinavian painters of the mid-nineteenth century and on into the emergence of modernism in the late 1920s. From the power of the region's rich landscape palette and geological and topographical characteristics to its often inclement weather, Scandinavian painters bring one closer to the Nordic world, articulating the full range of moods revealed and celebrated through their paintings.

Fig. 1.5 The city of Helsinki illustrates how the Nordic city adjusts to its natural setting of forest, rock and water. This aerial view from the Olympic Stadium tower (1938) *(see* Fig. 3.11) overlooks Töölö Bay and the Finnish National Opera House (1993) by Eero Hyuvyamyaki, Jukka Karhunen and Risto Parkkinena. (Photo: Krysta Mae Dimick)

The differing qualities found in each Nordic landscape can be observed in paintings embracing the larger natural characteristic of each. Small and intimate Denmark appears a vast land due to its undulating ridges, hills and varied views capped by the blue vault of the sky and theatre of the clouds. Jens Juel's realistic *A Storm Brewing behind a Farmhouse* (c. 1793), Johan Frederik Varmehren's *Study of the Heathland* (1854), and Vilhelm Hammershøi's *Landscape from Lejre* (1905) capture the intimate, meandering landscape of Denmark. In contrast, Norway has been described as an enormous rock keel stretching the length of the country and riven with valleys. Nature's drama of mountains, rivers, glaciers and fjords is captured by Norwegian artists and portrayed in powerful works such as Carl Johan Fahlcrantz's *The Waterfall at Trollhättan* (1828); J.C. Dahl's *Norwegian Mountain Landscape* (1819), *View from Lyshornet* (1836) and *View of Jostedalsbreen* (1844); Peder Balke's *View of Jostedalsbreen* (c. 1840s) and *From Nordland* (1850); August Cappelen's *Waterfall in Lower Telemark*

(1852); and Harald Sohlberg's *Flower Meadow in the North* (1905).

Sweden is a large and continuous land: the lower portion weaves land and water together and then the continuous forests and rolling hills are followed by the mountainous region of the far north. This range of landscape characteristics are seen in Alfred Wahlberg's *Swedish Landscape: A View from Kolmården* (1866); Niels Bjørnson Møller's *Mountain Landscape with Tourists* (1894); and Helmer Osslund's *Autumn* (1907). Finland is an interwoven network of lakes and continuous forests. It is far more uniform than Sweden and Norway and while Denmark is soft and smiling, Finland is hard and infecund. Water plays an essential role in the Finnish landscape, as seen in Albert Edelfelt's *Kaukola Ridge at Sunset* (1889) (Fig. 1.6) and Eero Järnefelt's *Autumn Landscape from Pielisjärvi* (1899).

While the forest with its percolating light impacts the Nordic view of the world, there are several types of forests in Scandinavia. The deciduous forests of Denmark are seen in C.W. Eckersberg's *Forest Study*

Fig. 1.6 Albert Edelfelt's *Kaukola Ridge at Sunset* (1905) illustrates a mood or atmosphere found in the Finnish landscape created by the forest, the sky and clouds and their reflection in the lake. (Photo: Albert Edelfelt [Public domain], via Wikimedia Commons. Located in the Ateneum Art Museum, Helsinki, Finland)

from Dyrehaven (1825) and Godfred Christensen's landmark work *A Spring Day at Herlufsholm* (1876); the birch groves throughout the North are captured in Victor Westerholm's *The Birch Grove* (1888); and the pine and fir forests are rendered in Prince Eugen's *The Forest* (1892) and Pekka Halonen's *Wilderness* (1899). The forest's irregular ground plane is presented in Marcus Larson's *Stony Forest Landscape* (1853).

The ever-changing Scandinavian sky with its theatric cloud formations is caught in Ferdinand von Wright's *Storm in Haminanlahti* (1857); Lars Hertervig's *View of Borgøya* (1867); Hans Gude's *Sandvik Fjord* (1879); Karl Nordström's *Storm Clouds* (1893); Prince Eugen's *The Old Castle* (1983) and *The Cloud*

(1895); and three powerful paintings by August Strindberg: *The Night in Jealousy* (1893), *Central Landscape* (1903) and *The Town* (1903).

The differing nature of Nordic light, be it the continuous daylight of the summer's midnight sun to the dark vault of the winter night, is expressed with great care in a full range of artistic works (*see* 'The 'Blue Hour': Summer Evenings on the South Beach of Skagen'). The midnight sun of summer is captured in Christian Skredsvig's *Summer Night, Moonlight in Nordmarken* (1884); also in female artist Kitty Kielland's *Summer Night* (1886) and Eilif Peterssen's *Summer Night* (1886), both capturing the summer light with water; and Richard Bergh's iconic pastoral *Nordic Summer Evening* (1900). The varying

There is a time during the midsummer evening at the beach in the Danish coastal town and art colony of Skagen where the sky and the sea seem to merge into each other in the same shade of blue. This twilight hour, the so called 'blue hour' occurs roughly around 10.00pm when the low summer sun dissolves into a blue atmospheric haze. Several artists from this period were engrossed in depicting this evocative blue transition between day and night in their paintings.

The most sensational of the works is Peder Severin Krøyer´s *Summer Night on the South Beach at Skagen, with Anna Ancher and Marie Krøyer* (1893) (Fig. 1.7), presenting the two artists going for an after-dinner stroll on the beach in the blue twilight. Krøyer captured the 'blue hour' in terms of both mood and colour; when the sky and the sea seem to merge into each other in the same shade of blue. The painting is the epitome of the idea of the artists' life in Skagen and the famous exceptional light in that particular place. Several of his works are titled the same *Summer Night on the South Beach at Skagen*, but then subtitled *The Artist's Wife and Dog by the Shore* (1892) and *The Artist and His Wife* (1899). In these three works a particular natural phenomenon or mood has been captured in an extraordinary way, providing a vivid understanding of a unique and special Northern condition.

In the winter there is another blue light, one that comes from darkness. It is an afternoon light illuminating the snow tunnels and castles built and used by children as they return home from school or at play. The memory of this light and its significance has been described by the Finnish architect Vesa Honkonen.[13]

Fig. 1.7 Peder Severin Krøyer's *Summer Night on the South Beach at Skagen, with Anna Ancher and Marie Krøyer* (1893) captures the 'Blue Hour' at about 10.00pm on a midsummer evening in the Danish seaside town of Skagen. (Photo: (aus meinem Archiv – Gratia Artis (trademark)) [Public domain], via Wikimedia Commons. Located in the Skagens Museum, Skagen, Denmark)

qualities of the winter night sky are expressed in Eugène Jansson's *Hornsgatan at Night* (1902) and in three exceptional works by Harald Sohlberg – *Night Glow* (1893), *Night* (1904) and *Winter Night in Rondane* (1914) (*see* Fig. 1.4).

Fjords, rivers, lakes and the sea play an essential role in the North. Not only does one travel on water, but water enhances mood in the Scandinavian world, especially when it is in play with particular qualities of light (*see* Fig. 1.3). Water provides reflections and ripples as well as shimmering in the light. The range of moods created by water are captured in August Cappelen's *Waterfall in Lower Telemark* (1852); Ferdinand von Wright's *Storm in Haminalahti* (1857); Hans Gude's *Sandvik Fjord* (1879); Anders Zorn's *Outdoors* (1888); Albert Edelfelt's *Kaukola Ridge at Sunset* (1889) (*see* Fig. 1.6); Akseli Gallen-Kallela's *Waterfall at Mäntykoski* (1894); Carl Wilhelmson's shimmering *Scene for the Swedish West Coast* (1898); Otto Hesselbom's national symbol, *Our Country* (1902); Eero Järnefelt's *Lake Shore with Reeds* (1905); and Gustaf Fjaestad's *Freshwater* (1905) and sparkling *Winter Evening by a River* (1907).

It would not be the North without snow and ice; a world captured in Frits Thaulow's *Winter* (1886); Carl Larsson's *The Open-Air Painter* (1886); Gustaf Fjaestad's *Hoar Frost on Ice* (1901); and Akseli Gallén-Kallela's *Landscape under Snow* (1902). In these paintings the artists capture, explore and celebrate the moods and atmospheres permeating the Scandinavian world, providing a richer understanding of the particular natural phenomena experienced by its inhabitants.

A Rural Past

Owing to its isolated geographical position off the beaten track of Europe, Scandinavia did not find itself part of the recurring invasions sweeping across Europe after the fall of the Roman Empire. It was the last region of Europe to be Christianized and that was during the late Middle Ages. Comparisons with other high-latitude regions of the world show that humans would have gained little more than a toehold in most of Scandinavia if it had not been for the westerly and south-westerly winds blowing across the Atlantic and the relatively warm waters of the Gulf Stream flowing beneath them.

While Denmark is at the same latitude as central Scotland, the other countries of the region stretch so far towards the Arctic that much of the territory, which looms large on the map of Europe, was sparsely inhabited or uninhabitable (*see* Figs 0.1 and 1.1). Deeply penetrating frost, long-continued snow cover and complete winter darkness are handicaps for which the much-advertised midnight sun of the summer can be modest compensation. Agriculture was further restricted by the poor average soil quality.

It was in this challenging geographical environment the Scandinavians found themselves in when they stopped wandering and became sedentary. In this formidable world they developed their attachment to the place, carved out their world and addressed nature. The Scandinavian urge to be in close communion with nature can be partly explained by the survival of a rural society into the twentieth century. A strong relationship with the elements developed from aeons of living in the wilderness; closely bound to the seasons and weather, and often immersed in darkness and ice, which are overcome each spring with the returning sun. The low population density of these lands is in itself another feature that characterizes the relationship between people and nature, influencing the very form of their settlements.

Unlike the South, where the piazza or plaza was the place of gathering and socializing, in the North domestic space provided for social get-togethers and communal activities. It is the home that entails intimacy and warmth. The significance of this is seen in both Nordic vernacular domestic architecture and in Scandinavian paintings of traditional life and endeavours (Fig. 1.8). Until the end of the nineteenth

Fig. 1.8 The farm courtyard was an important social and gathering space in Nordic vernacular farm complexes, as seen in Anders Zorn's illustrious painting *Midsummer Dance* (1897). The significance of the midsummer festival is celebrated by the tall maypole in the courtyard. (Photo: Anders Zorn [Public domain], via Wikimedia Commons. Located at the National Museum, Stockholm, Sweden)

century the most widespread form of urban aggregation was often the farmstead, the central element of the social and economic structure of the North. Isolated in remote valleys, found in forest clearings, or located on undulating hills and plains, the farmstead communicated human intervention in nature; a sense of civilization no matter how modest. Due to their environmental and social condition Scandinavians, unlike their Mediterranean counterparts, developed a model of life based on isolation rather than sociability. Each farmstead was a microcosm capable of functioning in a completely independent manner. Organized social life in its urban form, as it developed in continental Europe, is a relatively recent Nordic phenomenon generally restricted to the twentieth century.

Nordic Vernacular Architecture: Creating Place in the Forest

Architecture is tied to location, as site is an essential ingredient in its conception; it provides both corporeal and existential substance. Traditional Scandinavian architecture always exhibited a sense of measure, or appropriateness to place and users. The aim was to create an environmental and social microcosm for living; a considered, human response to nature's hardness and power. Norwegian painter J.C. Dahl captures how traditional farm complexes provided this sense of measure and created place in the dramatic Norwegian landscape in his iconic painting *View from Stalheim* (1842) and his later *View from Hjelle in Valdres* (1851). In these works one senses

Fig. 1.9 Fyrkat Møllegaard (c. 1600) in Hobro exemplifies Danish half-timbered construction which was used to build single-storeyed farm complexes with figurative thatched roof forms. The four-winged farm complex also has a watermill. (Photo: By Frank Vincentz (Own work) [GFDL (http://www.gnu.org/copyleft/fdl.html) or CC-BY-SA-3.0 (http://creativecommons.org/licenses/by-sa/3.0/)], via Wikimedia Commons)

the isolation of rural life, the immediacy to nature and the farmstead as a self-contained social and agricultural unit.

While the landscape characteristics of each country have different qualities, a number of architectural responses were similar. Establishing place required two acts: the first was to clear a space in the landscape in which to build; the second was to create a place for human action by establishing a courtyard or farmyard around which to organize the complex of buildings. The *gård*, *tun* or yard established the settlement by defining a place in the natural surroundings that provided both protection and the sense of community; protection from the elements and unwanted intruders while forming the centre of social life. Its creation humanized and civilized nature for the rural inhabitant and, importantly, was also the centre of agricultural life. The social importance of the courtyard is seen in paintings like Alexander Lauréus's *Peasant Dance at Christmas in Finland* (1815); Kilian Zoll's *Midsummer Dance at Rättvik* (1852); Eero Järnefelt's *Farmer and Farmhands*

(1893); Anders Zorn's famous *Midsummer Dance* (1897) (Fig. 1.8) and Tyko Sallinen's *The Country Dance* (1918).

Danish farm complexes are closed *firlænge* – a four-winged or four-sided courtyard farm. Nearness to nature is demonstrated through how the buildings adapt to topographic movement and rhythm. The farm buildings are typically of one storey, combining a half-timbered construction system with strong figurative roof forms of thatch. The house is embedded in the larger complex of buildings that surround the courtyard. Half-timbering creates a skeleton of horizontal and vertical wooden frames which can be infilled with windows, doors and materials such as brick or stucco (Fig. 1.9). Whereas Danish architecture had its roots in half-timbering, Swedish traditional architecture is defined by interlocking log construction, as in Finland and Norway. The Swedish farm complex is organized around a rectangular yard with the house expressed as a unit independent from the farm buildings. Resulting from the interlocking log construction, a sense of 'wall-ness' occurs through

Few other buildings express the Nordic world in the manner the Norwegian *stavkirke* or stave church does (Fig. 1.10), for it evolved as a unique structure with no parallel in Scandinavia. In a country carved from glaciers, these wooden medieval churches of Norway appear as natural outcroppings within a powerful landscape, growing directly out of their austere northern geography. Standing in a valley threatened by avalanches, with bare mountains towering above and a green glacier-fed stream or fjord below, it seems clear these buildings could not be at home anywhere but in this severe Norwegian landscape.

To approach a Norwegian stave church is to be overwhelmed by the feeling that the structure is alive. Rising out of the landscape, with carved dragon heads on its eave ends, the church conveys a mythical power like the serpent-dragon of Viking tales. It was an original architectural creation for which a native tradition was a prerequisite; in this case, the tradition of Viking shipbuilding. In a country where wooden churches were built in variance to canonical law, it is understandable that the form was unlikely to follow established ecclesiastical models or appearances. The builders exhibited a freedom and skill in the manner

they blended their rich Viking zoomorphic art and shipbuilding traditions with interpretations of church customs, creating both a unique form and spatial ambience.

Stave and interlocking log construction are the two methods that form the basis of Norwegian wooden architecture. These methods suggest how architectonic form can be simultaneously vertical and light through stave construction and horizontal and heavy through interlocking log techniques. The builders fashioned structural features to create unique forms and spatial effects previously unachieved in wood architecture. The use of vertical stave construction provides the height to the building, while the sloped, stepped, shingled roof metaphorically gives the impression of dragon scales.

In describing the transient quality of light in the North, it has been noted that only on winter nights is the sky large and unified, filled with 'dark light'. The stave church reifies this light: in its interior, the tall heavenward structural masts are lost in the reaches of upper darkness, where small peep-holes, tiny clerestory openings, illuminate the space like stars. This was a mystical space bringing the pagan past into assimilation with the Christian present and future.

Fig. 1.10 The stave church in Borgund, Norway (c. 1180–1250), illustrates that these churches were truly unique works of wooden architecture. The scale-like shingles and dragon-head roof ornaments makes the church appear practically alive. (Photo: Author)

Fig. 1.11 These farm buildings from the Setesdal region of Norway, now at the Norsk Folkemuseum in Oslo, illustrate the expressive nature of vertical, or stave, log construction. The loft on the far end is from Ose (c. 1700) while the three-part farmhouse is from Åmlid (late seventeenth century). (Photo: By Roede (Own work) [CC0], via Wikimedia Commons)

the expression of surface and mass in the buildings. Until the nineteenth century, farm complexes were usually left unpainted, but at that time a copper by-product became available: Falun red pigment. The sense of 'wall-ness' was intensified by painting the entire complex the colour red; a distinguishing feature of numerous farm complexes throughout Sweden.

Finnish vernacular architecture is closely related to Swedish influences, resulting from the influence of Swedish rule. But there is a division in the characteristics seen in Finnish farm complexes, one that corresponds to the country's own divisions into coastal and inland regions. Inland and eastwards towards Russia, log construction holds its own, with less formal groupings of farm buildings. Coastally and in the south-west, Swedish characteristics prevail, including painting the buildings Falun red. There were also the Karelian complexes (now primarily in Russia), with living quarters and haylofts forming an upper storey over cow stalls and storage rooms below. A unique element in Finnish farm complexes was the sauna, which was often the first building constructed.

While used for personal hygiene, it also was a place for birthing, family rituals and, as continues today, an important social space.

The central courtyard is essential to traditional dwelling complexes in Norway too. Even more than the neighbouring countries, Norwegian farm complexes read as small villages organized around a *tun*, the human courtyard and an animal courtyard. On the Norwegian farm the *tun* was a meeting place for life's most auspicious events; marriage, birth, death and special social occasions. While interlocking log construction was of primary importance, the continued use of stave construction acts as an essential feature in the creation of form and decoration in Norwegian vernacular architecture (Fig. 1.11). In contrast to the horizontality of log construction, the Norwegians continued to use the vertical stave technique, leading to an evocative interplay between the two, resulting in a rich variety of architectural expression. Within the farm complex the loft or storage house often best exemplifies the integration of log and stave constructions.

In contrast to the South, Nordic domestic space provided for social get-togethers and other family and community activities. The traditional Scandinavian dwelling was conceived as a heated place in the sub-arctic world, a place that entails intimacy and warmth. We see the significance of the living and dining space, as the space for social activity, in Scandinavian paintings of traditional life and social activities: R.V. Ekman's *Pistol Tells a Soldier's Tale: Scenes from Runneberg's 'Christmas Eve'* (1846) and *Folk Poet Pentti Lyytinen Reading His Works* (1848); Bengt Nordenberg's *A Tithe Meeting in Scania* (1865); Venny Soldaan-Brofeldt's *Meal in a Peasant Farmhouse in Savo* (1892); Pekka Halonen's *The Meal* (1899); and Jean Heiberg's *Afternoon Break* (1916).

Because Scandinavia remained a rural society into the twentieth century and closely tied to the world of the forest as witnessed in Nordic vernacular architecture, the region retains an intimacy with wood that continues to resonate in the Nordic soul. The importance of building in wood within the challenging forest landscape is captured in Akseli Gallen-Kallela's *Building* (1903). As Finnish architect Reima Pietilä said: 'There are two kinds of caves, caves of stone and caves of wood. The caves of wood are the dream of the people of the forest.'[14] In Nordic vernacular buildings one finds interiors where the log construction continues up from the walls to form the ceiling as well: a continuous space of wood. The wood vaults of Finnish churches of the late 1700s, among other examples, likewise express this desire for a cave-like interior: creating a sense of sky, their vaults' smoother surfaces contrast the heavy timber walls. (For a contemporary interpretation of a cave of wood, see Fig. 7.10.)

The concept of creating place in the Nordic landscape articulates one of the main characteristics informing Scandinavian architecture even today. For over a century and a half, Scandinavian architecture has been celebrated by both national and international writers for emphasizing its 'naturalness', its 'honest' use of materials, the clarity of its material composition and a particular affinity to place. The vernacular architecture of the North, from stave churches to farm complexes, provides important models on how a traditional people carved place out of a dramatic and harsh environment and creatively used their limited natural resources to make dwelling and dwellings possible. These characteristics form the basis of examining modern Scandinavian architecture.

Architecture, Place and Materiality

Architecture tells how we view the world and how we view ourselves in that world. As a reflection of cultural identity, Nordic architecture is more than a physical manifestation of materials and shapes, or of technological, political and economic conditions. It is also about how architecture represents a living, culturally anchored people in the world. The task of architecture is to enable dwelling and this is satisfied by building in resonance with a given place; that is, to make a site become a place that one relates to, identifies with and inhabits.

Nordic architecture is often presented as a realization of a northern *genius loci*, a seemingly natural response to the rough wilderness of the far North. To be sure, Scandinavian architecture is informed, inspired and conceived in relationship with nature and often wonderfully situated in ideal natural sites. Nordic buildings often do appear to grow naturally from the native soil and translate local forces and qualities into physical form. Simultaneously rooted and innovative, these buildings and complexes appear to bring out the essence of this locus: an architecture of the 'true North' shaped by climate, light or its absence, material resources and our perceptions of the arctic latitudes as to constitute its own regional construct. Modern and contemporary Scandinavian architecture follows in a long, remarkable and continuous tradition in which the topographical, geographical and climatic specificity of place seemingly constitutes an imperative for architecture and is a measure of its authenticity.

When speaking of Nordic building, place acts as a starting point for discussion. The character of Nordic architecture derives from the profound relationship between the building and the particular place it is located; that is, directly with the specific landscape and site. In the North, where nature essentially means woods, habitation is realized by means of 'making room', the initial act by humans in the realization of establishing place. The aim is to create a controllable, considered, human response to Nature's hardness, a micro-world to inhabit. This often meant creating a clearing to make a space or place within the forest. Nordic architecture seldom loses control of its context or the sense of appropriateness to the specific place and its inhabitants.

Nordic architects, in responding to the particulars of the ethereal Northern light and the harsh climate, have traditionally favoured an architectural expression of simple volumes. The buildings have a sense of tranquillity and quiet dignity through the use of unadorned materials, direct volumetric expression and removal of unnecessary decoration. The sense of restraint comes from a rural life of geographical seclusion on the edge of Europe, where one comes to terms with the solitude of an arctic climate. In addition, responding to the quality and character of light in Scandinavia, a variety of creative architectural forms have been developed that closely link important spaces with the sky. These forms are able to collect, preserve and allocate the scant illumination (*see* Figs 2.10, 4.4, 5.17, 6.5, 6.14 and 7.10).

Scandinavia as a rural society was closely tied to the world of the forest and the architecture retains an intimacy by using wood that continues to resonate in the Nordic psyche. Nordic vernacular buildings were generally of a single material: wood. This represents the most modest form of expression; construction based on a single material whose constant texture clearly exposes the shifting angles of the moving sun (*see* Figs 1.8, 1.10, 1.11 and 2.2). In addition to wood, another traditional material widely employed in the Nordic lands to bring a self-assured modesty to building is brick. It is often expressed as bare, tactile walls

that stand on their own, free of adornment. The use of yellow brick in Denmark and red brick in Finland exemplifies this (*see* Figs 4.2, 5.2, 5.3, 5.14 and 5.16). A more recent example of the expressive power found in using a single material is seen in the Scandinavian concrete churches of the 1960s and 1970s (*see* Figs 5.13, 5.15, 5.18 and 6.5).

There is often a white luminosity present in the interior spaces of Scandinavian civic, commercial and religious buildings that is a direct response to the arctic climate. The white finish allows spaces to remain lit even in the dark winter with its snow-covered landscapes. White rooms offer a means to stay near the most elusive aspects of nature, the delicate daylight and unpredictable weather. In the domestic setting, Vilhelm Hammershøi's iconic painting *Dust Motes Dancing in Sunlight* (1900), along with his *Interior with a Lady* (1901), *Open Doors (White Doors)* (1905) and *Interior with Punchbowl* (1907) capture this existential quality, as does Anna Ancher's *The Maid in the Kitchen* (1886). The importance of capturing the allusive sunshine is seen in the white interiors of Scandinavian medieval church interiors, as well as numerous religious, civic, institutional and commercial buildings from the nineteenth century to the present day (*see* Figs 4.4, 4.5, 6.5 and 6.14).

Today, at one level, Nordic architecture appears to continue to emphasize its 'naturalness', 'honest' use of materials and particular affinity to place. This view has remained the primary way Scandinavian architecture is presented and assessed. It presumes that Nordic architecture continues to be responsive to geographical particularities of the northern latitudes while simultaneously responding to the society in which it is situated. Today a new generation of architects is proposing more interesting relationships to place than just responsiveness to geography and topography, or the use of local materials

While Nordic architects in recent years have grappled anew with brick, wood, granite, concrete, glass and steel as important materials for a building culture that draws on their major designers of the twentieth century, they are attempting to add something new where those architects left off. While this may speak of a modern regionalism, recent Nordic architecture is not primarily about returning to traditional customs, but rather about using geographically determined qualities in new ways. This could be seen as a statement for a new generation of architects rebelling against a perceived 'tyranny of place' as defined by the past. These architects are seeking to cultivate a more sophisticated and many-layered meaning of nature and place. Through a vigorous exchange of ideas and images, today's architecture is becoming influenced more by global movements than by local building customs (*see* Figs 7.1, 7.4, 7.5, 7.6, 7.7, 7.12, 7.13 and 7.14). As is becoming common throughout the world, societies are increasingly acting globally, often disengaging from local traditions.

The Welfare State and Architecture

During the twentieth century, the Scandinavian countries developed similarly constructed welfare states, in which social services are distributed in an egalitarian and uniform way. The Nordic welfare model is generally perceived as an extensive and well-organized civil administration that is active on a local, regional and national level. It is financed through public funding and the taxation of its citizens. Rather than speaking of a 'welfare state', which may imply social assistance and long-term dependency on that state, today many prefer the term 'social investment state'. What this term suggests is that spending on education, health-care and other social services should not be viewed as expenses that drag down the economy but as investments that eventually pay great dividends for society as a whole.

A foundation of the cultural and political manifestation of the welfare state was an enthusiastic embrace of modernity in all its forms, including architecture, planning and furniture and product designs because of their rational development and functionality. From the time of the 1930 Stockholm Exhibition onwards (*see* Figs 3.1 and 3.5), modernity

and state social programmes were inextricably linked. Both the social and architectural realizations came to represent the Nordic nations as progressive peoples of the future.

The principles of the Nordic model were secured by a large state or state-supported sector that subsidized industrialization by building housing for workers, as well as buildings for education, culture, child- and eldercare and sports and recreation in large numbers. The architectural ideas of modernism were put to work to realize the societal vision that combined with local preconditions – like building traditions, materials and climate – to create a unique form of modern architecture.

A common feature of modern Nordic architecture is the humanist foundation on which the welfare society is based, especially as realized in the state-supported cultural, health and educational institutions. Here one finds a combination of social values, awareness of resources and building processes influencing modern and contemporary Nordic architecture. A number of new public and civic buildings in Scandinavia demonstrate how the welfare model, for more than half a century the fulcrum of political and cultural developments, constantly informs architecture and planning principles and progress.

With the evolution of the welfare state and its concomitant urbanization, coupled with the focus on quality housing development supported by government engagement, the city became the preferred place for living in the North. But this was a new kind of city – clean, full of light, responsive to nature and its exigencies. Trees, rivers, lakes and rock outcroppings abound in these cities and it is 'around' these places that the Nordic city forms and develops; it is around natural elements that the urban tissue grows, like the farmsteads of the past and their making of place (*see* Figs 1.5, 6.11 and 7.9). There is light and air and a lot of greenery in the welfare city and this was a break with the then normative types of urban spaces, such as streets, markets and squares, which formed both the historical and early industrial cities in the South.

The Architectural Competition

There is another tradition that has contributed to the high quality of Scandinavian architecture: selection of public architectural commissions by using government-sponsored architectural competitions. The practice of selecting public commissions by architectural competition developed in the late nineteenth century and was seen as a democratic process that not only identified the best designs but also fostered an experimental tradition where new architectural ideas could be presented and new talent exposed. This is especially important for young architects for it allows them to compete with established architects on an equal footing. And more than once, an architectural student has won a major building commission. Competitions contributed a sense of ethical and fiscal responsibility to the larger society and part of a public process in which the best ideas conceivably thrived.

When American architect Paul Spreiregen stated that 'of all the countries employing competitions, the Scandinavian countries have enjoyed the most success with them',[15] it is implicit that the Nordic competitions have managed that delicate balance of advocating an experimental, artistic tradition and maintaining a dialogue with the public. Of the buildings discussed in this book, the vast majority were commissioned through competitions. From Eliel Saarinen and Ragnar Östberg, to Arne Jacobsen and Alvar Aalto, to Sverre Fehn and Reima Pietilä and to contemporary architectural firms like BIG and Snøhetta, competitions have played a major role in securing their work and demonstrating both building competency and design experimentation. Moreover, they spurred lively competition between rivals, resulting in an active, engaged architectural community and informed public.

The Nordic countries have used the architectural competitions in the most efficient manner to realize new buildings and urban design projects: over 80 per cent of public buildings in Denmark, Finland and Norway and over 70 per cent of new works in Sweden being chosen through competitions. Interestingly, many contemporary public entities and private clients throughout the world have taken a page from the Nordic playbook and actively use architectural competitions as a primary means of architect selection. For practising Nordic architects today, one only has to look at their webpages to see the number of national, regional and international competitions they have entered. This has played an important role in the dissemination of Northern architectural ideas and concepts globally and has provided Scandinavian architects with a level of worldwide recognition they well deserve.

Post-Second World War suburban development in Scandinavia solidified this vision in numerous projects. Outside Stockholm two model new towns were built, Vällingby (1947–54) (*see* Fig. 5.1) and Farsta (1956–60); and the iconic Tapiola (1949 onwards) (*see* Fig. 6.16) was developed outside Helsinki. The British garden-city movement, which was sensitive to topography and landscape, was melded with the rational modern planning needs required by the welfare state. These developments had densely populated activity centres housing a central subway station and integrated housing and work. At the same time, nature intruded into the compositions: boulders, pines and birches and water helped give the places a unique atmosphere that did not exist anywhere else in the world. This model of development has informed Nordic planning projects for the past sixty years and continues to do so.

Today, for the outside observer, even a passing assessment of the designs for culture, education,

Fig. 1.12 The Oslo Opera House by Snøhetta (2007) exemplifies new civic buildings in Scandinavia. Being located along the waterfront, it is not only a cultural institution and part of a public promenade but provided the catalyst for the development of the Bjørvika neighbourhood in central Oslo following its construction (see Fig. 7.13). (Photo: Krysta Mae Dimick)

childcare and performance demonstrates the ongoing vitality of modernity and its realizations across the Nordic region. Indeed, the contemporary moment in Scandinavian architecture can be characterized as a 'Renaissance' in public and civic design, as well as housing and commercial architecture. But it is the buildings for culture, education and community that are in the foreground, as witnessed in the water-front developments in the Nordic capitals and larger cities. Emblematic of the vitality and effectiveness of these new cultural entities are the opera houses, symphony halls and museums located on the harbours, water-ways and lakes of Oslo, Copenhagen, Helsinki and Stockholm (see Figs 1.5, 1.12, 6.11, 6.16, 7.2 and 7.5).

In addition to being iconic architectural works these buildings have become important places of public and civic engagement and participation.

In Scandinavia as elsewhere, globalization is having its impact and influence on society as well as architecture. The questions are there: How will the welfare state address immigration and changing demographics? Will architects continue to maintain a sense of regional identification in the work or not? And if so, how will it manifest itself? The next chapters examine the influence of modernity on the evolution of Nordic architecture, how it was interpreted and reinterpreted over the past 100-plus years and continues to be today.

Chapter 2

THE JOURNEY TO MODERNISM:
A ROMANTIC AND CLASSICAL VOYAGE

TOWARDS THE END OF THE NINETEENTH and beginning of the twentieth centuries a growth of national self-awareness occurred in Scandinavia; a self-awareness stimulated by archaeological discoveries that increased awareness of the important role Scandinavians played in the distant and recent past. This included a deeper understanding of the Stone, Bronze and Iron Ages, the Vikings and their voyages of exploration and colonization, the conversion to Christianity during the Middle Ages and Nordic engagements in the greater European sweep of history (such as the Reformation, Thirty Years' War and the Enlightenment).

Scandinavian nationalism was also fostered by changing political and social developments. First, living conditions in Scandinavia were improving as a result of new means of agricultural production coupled with increased industrial and commercial development. The second factor was the growth of democratic institutions and development of better means of communication, via rail, telephone and postal services, into the rural countryside. The third was the position of women in Northern society: they were able to vote, access a variety of jobs and attend gender-integrated schools (*see* 'Women Architects in Early Twentieth-Century Finland'). Lastly, resulting from the concomitant urban migration, Scandinavia was transforming from its rural traditions into a progressive modern urban society with an emerging middle class. While these developments created a sense of national focus in each Nordic country, for Norway and Finland this also meant seeking national independence. Norway peacefully separated from Sweden in 1905, while Finland declared independence

from Russia in 1917, though this was followed by civil war.

Nordic architects were influenced by the contemporaneous work of Scandinavian archaeologists and art and architectural historians. The stone churches and secular buildings of the Romanesque period were considered to be particularly 'Northern', thus appropriate 'national' references for architectural expression (*see* Fig. 6.12). Understanding of these works was gained through doing direct field documentation of the extant buildings. Many of the major medieval religious buildings in Scandinavia were also undergoing preservation and restoration. The other unique 'Northern' tradition was the wooden churches and vernacular farm complexes found throughout the region, which were also documented (*see* Figs 1.9, 1.10 and 1.11). This interest in folk architecture resulted in the development of Scandinavian folk museums which brought buildings from the country to 'open-air museums' in the cities. At this time the Norsk Folkemuseum (1894) in Oslo, Skansen (1891) in Stockholm, the Frilandsmuseet (1897) in Copenhagen and Seurasaari (1909) in Helsinki were established. These museums featured vernacular buildings and complexes containing traditional furniture and applied designs, with guides dressed in folk costumes, allowing the urban dweller to recall the authenticity and simplicity of the rural past.

Simultaneously the influence of the middle class was increasing and with power waning from the nobility there was increasing focus on buildings for democratic institutions. Universities, schools, libraries and, importantly, town halls emerged as significant public building types. The role of the

While Scandinavian artists sought to create works based upon expressing national cultural origins and themes, resulting in the National Romantic movement, the complexity of cultural, social and environmental changes are witnessed in the subject matter found in Nordic painting. In capturing the specifics of Scandinavian geography, history, politics and landscape, several types of subject matter appeared: images of traditional and working-class activities, *plein-air* Nordic landscapes, celebration of the lifestyle of the middle class and meditations on the alienation fostered by industrialization and urbanization.

Interest in expressing traditional values and national cultural origins are seen in scenes of working-class and rural activities as exemplified by Anna Ancher's *Lars Gaihede Carving a Stick* (1880), Akseli Gallen-Kallela's *Boy* with a Crow (1884) and *Building* (1903), Peder Severin Krøyer's *In the Store during a Pause from Fishing* (1882), Laurits Andersen Ring's *In the Month of June* (1899), Erik Theodor Werenskiold's *On the Plain* (1883) and Anders Zorn's *Midsummer Dance* (1897) (*see* Fig. 1.8). Respect for the Nordic environment is seen in *plein-air* landscapes, including Albert Edelfelt's *Kaukola Ridge at Sunset* (1889) (*see* Fig. 1.6), Prince Eugen's *The Cloud* (1896), Gustaf Fjaestad's *Freshwater* (1905), Pekka Halonen's *Wilderness* (1899), Eero Järnefelt's *Lake Shore with Reeds* (1905), Eilif Peterssen's *Summer Night* (1886) and Otto Hesselbom's emblematic *Our Country* (1905).

Industrialization, changing social roles, modernization and urbanization promoted the emergence of the Scandinavian middle class with its resultant bourgeois culture and lifestyle. Simultaneously, there was also a growing alienation caused by these same forces. Harriet Backer's *Blue Interior* (1883), Richard Bergh's *Nordic*

Fig. 2.1 Edvard Munch's *Anxiety* (1894) captures the sense of alienation many experienced in the modernizing *fin-de-siècle* Nordic urban world. The painting provides an interesting comparison to the bourgeois life represented in Krøyer's *Summer Night on the South Beach at Skagen (see* Fig. 1.7). (Photo: Edvard Munch [Public domain], via Wikimedia Commons. Located in the Munch Museum, Oslo, Norway)

Summer Evening (1900), Peder Severin Krøyer's *Portrait of the Hirschsprung Family* (1891) and his Skagen series (*see* Fig. 1.7) (*see* 'The 'Blue Hour': Summer Evenings on the South Beach of Skagen'), Ellen Thesleff's *Violin Player* (1896), Edvard Munch's *A Spring Day on Karl Johan Street* (1890) and Helena Schjerbeck's *Girls Reading* (1900) capture this emergent middle class, while numerous works by Carl Larsson present a blissful vision of bourgeois family life.

In contrast, Edvard Munch's *Evening on Karl Johan Street* (1893), *Anxiety* (1894) (Fig. 2.1) and *The Dance of Life* (1900), Christian Krohg's *Struggle for Existence* (1889) and Marcus Collin's *Factory Girls* (1916), express the alienation experienced in the then modernizing Nordic urban world. For many, industrialization seemed to sever ties with nature, proposing that technological advances could create a better life for people than association with nature. This industrialization verses nature

duality would engage Nordic architects over the next century: from National Romanticism's wooden villa architecture enhancing contact with nature; to 1920s classicism attempting to humanize and civilize the Nordic landscape; to the critique of modernism by Erik Gunnar Asplund and Alvar and Aino Aalto; to the post-war period's relationships between building and locale; and finally to the question of the role of place in contemporary Nordic architecture.

city hall transformed as urban services increased and were concentrated therein and as new expectations and requirements emerged. As emblems of effective urban democracy, the city hall became in the hands of the National Romantic architects a new kind of 'people's house', accessible to all. Stockholm, Oslo and Copenhagen all built new, iconic and architecturally powerful city halls (*see* Figs 2.5, 2.6 and 6.11).

Social changes brought on by urbanization and industrialization resulted in new building types and increased work for architects. In addition to open-air folk museums, the importance of national archaeological and ethnographic collections created the need for the development of national museums; new museums were built in Stockholm, Oslo (*see* Fig. 2.3) and Helsinki. The rail, telephone and postal systems were expanding. Hundreds of new local train stations were built, as were depots in the major cities (*see* Fig. 2.9). Telephone company facilities expanded due to the increased presence of the telephone in daily life. New, larger post offices were built to respond to the ever-increasing mail service.

The Architecture of National Romanticism

Scandinavian National Romantic architecture began as a wood architecture that provided freer plan configurations, spaces and forms, including broad verandas with ornamented gables and incorporating larger window and door openings that allowed for enhanced contact between inside and outside. The architecture of National Romanticism also incorporated historic forms and decorative symbols of national identity: medieval churches, traditional farm complexes (*see* Figs 1.9 and 1.11) and Norwegian stave churches (*see* Fig. 1.10) provided formal inspiration for architects, while bears, pine cones, other flora and fauna and mythic Nordic creatures were incorporated into details and decorative motifs.

For the first time in the modern era, folk buildings provided a model for civic, commercial and domestic architecture. Why did late nineteenth-century Nordic society choose a folk typology for a design paradigm? There was the desire to be liberated from the formal, often classical, prototypes of church, palace and civic architecture. Vernacular architecture was rooted in values of daily life that were appreciated by the expanding middle class with its bourgeois lifestyle and witnessed in the popularity of the new folk and national museums. It represented closer contact with nature for those recent rural migrants now residing in the cities of the North, providing a counter to the alienation associated with industrialization and urbanization.

National Romantic buildings incorporated the formal characteristics of 'romantic architecture': they were picturesquely composed with irregular floor plans and with building mass and volume determining architectural character. Integration or reciprocity with site conditions replaced the classical preference of standing in contrast to nature. The material palette was quite tactile; granite or soapstone left uncut or roughly dressed, hand-moulded or specially made bricks and roofing tiles, and rough-hewn logs, wooden siding (cladding) and shingles. Irregular building masses and profiles were complemented by the use of heavily rusticated masonry surfaces, protruding log ends and numerous textural variations.

National Romantic buildings, like contemporaneous Continental works, were integrated entities with art, furnishings, craft and architecture merged into an expressive and consistent experiential whole. Influences included William Morris and the British Arts and Crafts movement, along with the architecture of Charles Rennie Mackintosh, Baillie Scott and Charles Voysey and the heavy Romanesque-inspired masonry masses and detailing of American architect Henry Hobson Richardson. Art nouveau and *Jugendstil* works were being produced on the Continent and they too had influence on Nordic developments.

Norway

Inspiration for architecture unmistakably Nordic was found in traditional Norwegian wooden architecture, particularly medieval stave churches and vernacular farm complexes (*see* Figs 1.10 and 1.11). As architect Hans Jacob Sparre wrote in 1901: 'It was as if Norway's traditional wooden architecture had grown out of our nature and our landscape, our mountains and forests … it was a place-specific building tradition, deriving from our own roots.'[16] This inspired a development known as the *dragestil* (dragon style), alluding to the dragon heads adorning the gables of stave churches. The leading exponent was Holm Munthe and while some of his works were destroyed by fire, the distinctive Frognerseteren Restaurant (1890) outside Oslo still stands. Nearby is the large Holmenkollen Park Hotel complex (1896) by Balthasar Lange, with its fantastic, colourful, exotic character (Fig. 2.2), and the restrained rural farm vernacular-influenced Royal Lodge (1911) by Kristian Hjalmar Biong.

Examples of *dragestil* churches include St Olaf's Church in Balestrand (1897) and the Vår Frue Church in Porsgrunn (1899) designed by Haldor Larsen Børve; and the Buksnes Church (1905) in Vestvågøy, the Veøy Church (1907) in Sølsnes and the Holm Church (1907) in Rauma designed by Karl Norum. Børve also designed the fantastical Dalen Hotel in Telemark (1894), one of the largest wooden buildings in Norway. At this time the Norwegian rail system was expanding and many new stations, designed by Paul Armin Due, were executed in a restrained *dragestil*.

Emancipation from Sweden in 1905 spurred a desire for a more Norwegian architecture for important civic buildings, liberating public architecture from the reigning nineteenth-century historicism. Three convincing public buildings were produced by architect Henrik Bull: the eclectic National Theatre (1899) in Bergen, and, in Oslo, the Historical Museum (1902) (Fig. 2.3) and the government administration building (1906) in its austere rusticated granite. Of the three, the Historical Museum is a sophisticated, progressive work which incorporated national motifs and materials with the flowing sensuous rhythms associated with art nouveau.

Other major public works include the Bergen Train Station (1913) by Jens Zetlitz Monrad Kielland, with its powerful stone front and cast-iron train shed; the

Fig. 2.2 Balthasar Lange's Holmenkollen Park Hotel (1896) exemplifies the colourful and referential wooden *dragestil* or dragon-style National Romantic architecture of Norway. (Photo: Author)

rough-cut stone Bergen Public Library (1906) by Olav Nordhagen; and the dramatic asymmetrical Trondheim Bank (1907) executed in rubble construction by Johan Osness. The Vålerenga Church (1902) in Oslo, by Heinrich Jürgensen and Holgar Sinding-Larsen, is memorable due to its powerful asymmetrically placed bell tower. Romanesque architecture and the work of American architect H.H. Richardson influenced the design of the Norwegian Institute of Technology (1910) in Trondheim by Bredo Greve.

An important building begun during this period but not completed until 1950 was the Oslo City Hall. The winning competition entry of 1916, by Magnus Poulsson and Arnstein Arneberg, proposed a stone castle formally echoing Oslo's Akershus Fortress overlooking the harbour. Due to economic and political issues, the building went through two redesign periods, so the original referential features were eventually stripped away (*see* Fig. 6.11). Inspired by art nouveau, the Havnelageret commercial building (1921) in Oslo by Bredo Henrik Berntsen was the largest concrete structure in Europe and the largest building in Scandinavia at the time of its construction.

One of the worst conflagrations to which wooden Norwegian towns were subjected to occurred in the city of Åselund in January 1904. The entire downtown was destroyed and, following a planning period, the town was rebuilt in stone, brick and stucco in the *Jugendstil*. The structures built between 1904 and 1907 were designed and built by some thirty Norwegian architects and twenty master builders, resulting in a unique and unusually distinctive urban form and consistent architecture ensemble.

Fig. 2.3 The Historical Museum (1902) in Oslo by Henrik Bull incorporates national motifs and materials with the flowing lines associated with the Continental art nouveau. (Photo: Author)

Sweden

Several Swedish architects worked towards the development of a national style using the *dragestil* as seen in Agi Lindegren's Biological Museum (1893) in Stockholm and Gustaf Wickman's Kiruna Church (1912). But the essence of Swedish National Romanticism is captured in several exemplary churches whose common features include brick construction, romantic volumetric massing, exaggerated bell towers creatively interpreting historic church tower forms, Baltic-style pediments and eave ends referencing the buildings of Stockholm's historic Gamla Stan quarter and medieval-inspired detailing.

Three works are in Stockholm. Lars Israel Wahlman's Engelbrekt Church (1914) (Fig. 2.4) rises dramatically from a rock promontory on a series of stone terraces that creates an expressive, complex exterior form. The interior and exterior surfaces are richly articulated with an eclectic collection of ornamentation and detail. The church forms the centre of the Lärkstaden district, a contemporaneous housing development planned by Per Olof Hallman. Both Carl Bergsten's Hjorthagen Church (1909) and Ivar Tengbom's massive Högalid Church (1923) incorporate romantically composed brick volumes with exaggerated, referential bell towers.

Outside Stockholm the dramatically sited Church of the Epiphany (1913) in Saltsjöbaden by Ferdinand Boberg has a monumental church tower and incorporates Baltic-style elements throughout. Near the church is the Storängen district, established in 1904, which contains a number of architect-designed National Romantic-style homes. The Masthugg

Fig. 2.4 Lars Israel Wahlman's Engelbrekt Church (1914) illustrates Swedish National Romantic architecture with its romantic composition, exaggerated bell tower and tactile materials. Placed on a rocky promontory it overlooks the contemporaneous housing development below. (Photo: By I99pema (Own work) [CC BY-SA 3.0 (http://creativecommons.org/licenses/by-sa/3.0)], via Wikimedia Commons)

Church in Gothenburg (1912) by Sigfrid Ericson, with romantically organized volumes surmounted by an over-scaled bell tower, rises emphatically on a cliff above the Göta River.

Carl Westman's Law Courts building (1915) in Stockholm, with continuous masonry walls accented with rhythmic windows and a strong central tower form, is modelled after Vadstena Castle. Westman's Röhsska Museum of Handicrafts (1914) in Gothenburg uses handmade red bricks and incorporates traditional Swedish roof forms. Cyrillus Johansson's apartment complex at Nybrogatan 11-13 (1912) in Stockholm is a large romantic composition executed in dark red handmade brick. Ferdinand Boberg created several significant works synthesizing traditional Swedish castle and tower forms with Baltic roof elements and constructed of handmade bricks: the Gävle Fire Station (1891), the Rosenbad building (1902) in Stockholm and the central post offices for Stockholm (1904) and Malmö (1906). His NK department store (1915), with its light-filled four-storey interior atrium, is *Jugendstil* in inspiration. The animated use of stone in Sweden's first public library, the Dickerson Public Library (1897) in Gothenburg by Hans Hedlund, was influenced by American architect H.H. Richardson.

As in the other Nordic countries, the expansion of the rail network resulted in numerous new stations being constructed. In the 1890s the design of stations, many by architect Erik Lallerstedt, become less

Fig. 2.5 The Stockholm City Hall (1923) by Ragnar Östberg is one of the most commanding city halls, not to mention civic buildings, constructed during the National Romantic period. (Photo: By Arild Vågen (Own work) [CC BCopenhagen CY-SA 3.0 (http://creativecommons.org/licenses/by-sa/3.0)], via Wikimedia Commons)

formal in execution, using free plans, asymmetrical façades and some domestic imagery.

In Stockholm, Isak Gustaf Clason and Kasper Salin's Stockholm Market Hall (1889) is a muscular expressive work with medieval references, while Clason's Nordic Museum (1907) realizes its national identity through recalling the Vasa period's Gripsholm Castle. Gustaf Wickman's rusticated red stone Skånes Enskilda Bank (1900) had an elegantly crafted banking hall while Axel Anderberg's Museum of Natural History (1916), outside Stockholm, is an extensive brick and stone ensemble. And what could be more nationalistic than an Olympic stadium? Torben Grut's stadium for the 1912 Stockholm Olympics draws its inspiration from buildings in Visby, a medieval Hanseatic seaport on the island of Gotland.

But Ragnar Östberg's Stockholm City Hall (1923) (Fig. 2.5) overshadows all other contemporaneous Swedish buildings. It is beautifully sited on the water's edge, with an asymmetrically placed over-scaled tower that dominates yet gathers together the sky, the water and surrounding city neighbourhoods. The massive red brick building is lightened with a granite colonnade and syncopated window treatment. But it is the dramatic, exquisitely detailed interior spaces of the building, including the Blue Hall, Golden Hall and Prince's Gallery, that move the visitor to awe. While incorporating numerous Nordic references within the building and its decorative designs, there is also a sense of the Venetian as it perches on the water and penetrates the sky. It is an elegant, sophisticated, powerful 'people's house'.

Denmark

In Denmark, the country's half-timbered construction tradition (*see* Fig. 1.9), the extensive use of brick with stone detailing (recalling medieval churches such as Roskilde Cathedral) and stepped gables on traditional church towers and building end walls all contributed to informing a national architectural identity and style. Martin Nyrop's Copenhagen City Hall (1905) (Fig. 2.6) represented an important break from the reigning classicism and historicism,

becoming a model for later Scandinavian city halls. The red brick building employs numerous references to medieval Danish architecture, as well as northern Italian ones. It is simultaneously monumental and inviting with numerous well-appointed public meeting and reception rooms, and, like its Oslo and Stockholm sisters, is a true 'house of the people'.

Of the buildings defining the City Hall plaza, there are two other important works: the Palace Hotel (1910) by Anton Rosen and the Hotel Bristol (1902) by Vilhelm Fischer. These three buildings, with their exaggerated towers and expressive brick façades, create an engaging ensemble of National Romantic architecture. Rosen also designed the art nouveau-inspired Løvenborg building (1906), with its richly decorated curtain wall, and the expressive

Fig. 2.6 Simultaneously monumental and inviting, Martin Nyrop's refined brick Copenhagen City Hall (1905) successfully synthesizes both Nordic and northern Italian architectural references. (Photo: By Scythian (Own work) [CC BY-SA 3.0 (http://creativecommons.org/licenses/by-sa/3.0) or GFDL (http://www.gnu.org/copyleft/fdl.html)], via Wikimedia Commons)

Fig. 2.7 The Grundtvig's Church (1921–40), by Peter Vilhelm Jensen-Klint, reinterprets the idea of Gothic architecture through its supersized yellow brick western façade; a façade that dwarfs its surrounding contemporaneous housing estate. (Photo: Krysta Mae Dimick)

commercial building at Vesterbrogade 40 (1909), both in Copenhagen.

Important works in Copenhagen include the Hotel Bethel (1906) and the medieval-inspired St Timothy Church (1911) by Jens Christian Kofoed, both executed in brick; Frits Koch's expressive Telephone Company headquarters (1909); a series of brick and stone commercial buildings by Eugen Jørgensen along Christian IX's Gade (1907); Emil Jørgensen's Romanesque-inspired Church of the Deaf (1904) and St Augustinus Church (1914); Andreas Fussing's Taastrup Water Tower (1908); and Ulrik Plesner and Aage Langeland-Mathiesen's apartment complex at 37–43 Vodroffsvej (1909).

Hack Kampmann executed exemplary works in northern Denmark, including the Customs House (1898), Theatre (1900) and St Johannes Church (1905), all in Aarhus, and Aalborg's Post Office (1910). These red brick buildings, with expressive stone and tile detailing, incorporate medieval references and roof forms. Heinrich Wenck, chief architect for the Danish State Railway, designed over 150 stations, from large urban stations, like the Copenhagen Central Station (1911) and Esbjerg Station (1904), to numerous small ones whose medieval forms and half-timbered construction reference Denmark's historic and traditional past.

A unique and expressionist work, the Grundtvig's Church by Peder Vilhelm Jensen-Klint was designed in 1913 but constructed between 1921 and 1940 (Fig. 2.7). With neo-Gothic references, the supersized stepped west façade overpowers the contemporaneously designed housing complex surrounding the church. Constructed of over six million yellow bricks, the building truly captures modern architect Mies van der Rohe's dictum about architecture beginning when two bricks are carefully laid upon each other.

The search for national identity was most fruitful in Finland, where National Romanticism was inextricably linked with the growth of Finnish nationalism, cultural awareness and the quest for political independence. While Finland's building traditions were more provincial than those of her neighbours, the new nation possessed a national source of inspiration for the arts: the *Kalevala*. Influencing all the arts, this epic poem formulated a complete cosmology and mythology that poetically explained the character of the Finnish countryside and its people.

Artist Akseli Gallén-Kallela's self-built log timber studio 'Kalela' (1895) and architect Lars Sonck's summer home (1895) were Finland's first National Romantic works. Gesellus, Lindgren and Saarinen's 'Hvitträsk' (1902), the architects' home and studio built outside Helsinki, incorporated a number of rural vernacular Finnish architectural motifs. Formed around a traditional farm courtyard, the romantic composition integrates medieval church towers with vernacular interlocking log architecture.

Stone is always close at hand in Finland and the desire to create a durable expression made it the preferred building material, as seen in two buildings by Gesellus, Lindgren and Saarinen in Helsinki. The Pohjola Insurance building (1901) is romantically composed and executed in rock-faced stone enhanced by decorative details with naturalistic and mythic associations. Their National Museum (1912) was a referential essay in stone synthesizing three Finnish historic motifs: a steep gable form ornamented as a medieval church, a round corner tower referencing medieval castles and an over-scaled church bell tower. The decorative details included Finnish flora and fauna.

In 1905 Lars Sonck designed the Helsinki Telephone building; its skilfully balanced asymmetric rough stone façade is contrasted by decorative incised geometrical ornamentation on polished granite columns. With its historical associations synthesized into an asymmetrical and picturesque composition and boldly executed in irregular, rusticated stone, Tampere Cathedral (1907) is Sonck's finest work (Fig. 2.8). The square plan has extended wall and support elements alluding to interlocking log construction. The interior detailing and art work is rich with associative qualities, reminding one of Finnish medieval churches. It is a work giving permanent form to the anticlassical; it is heavy, rough, atmospheric and mythic.

Onni Tarjanne's National Theatre (1902) in Helsinki and the Tampere Fire Station (1907) by female architect Wivi Lönn are also excellent works. Contemporaneously, there appeared a number of *Jugendstil*-inspired works in Finland: the Valtion Hotelli in Imatra (1903) by Usko Nyström, the Grand Hotel Börs (1908) in Tampere by F. Strandell, and numerous apartment buildings in Helsinki by Eliel Saarinen and his partners.

An important transition away from National Romanticism began with the completion of the Helsinki Central Railway Station (1914) by Eliel Saarinen (Fig. 2.9). The original competition entry of 1904 by Gesellus, Lindgren and Saarinen was a picturesque medieval-inspired composition. The design was heavily criticized by the younger generation of Finnish architects as being anachronistic and lacking a rational basis for the design. Sigurd Frosterus commented, 'To use archaic forms without real justification is as senseless as it would be to go around dressed in skins, eat with fingers, or shoot with bow and arrow instead of rifle.'[17] Gustaf Strengell noted, 'In Finland we no longer earn our living by hunting and fishing: floral ornamentation and bears – let alone other animals – are hardly representative of an age of steam and electricity.'[18] Saarinen completed the commission in the *Jugendstil*, which eschewed archaic references and was constructed of concrete, here used for the first time in a major Finnish public building.

A Light Repast: 1920s Nordic Classicism

Following the First World War, nationalistic expression was giving way to a more rational direction in the North. Nordic architects began embracing an abstract, lighter and purer form of expression, in essence turning towards classicism. With Frosterus and Strengell's comments alluding to the increasing modernity of Scandinavian life and architecture, buildings like Ferdinand Boberg's NK department store and Saarinen's Helsinki Central Railway Station (Fig. 2.9) were among the initial critical reactions to the idiosyncratic quality of National Romanticism. But two earlier works embraced classicism more fully. Lars Sonck's Helsinki Stock Exchange (1911) incorporated classical exterior expression, with an interior that creates an archetypal Scandinavian space. Sonck's internalized exterior space or atrium – a Northern plaza under glass – accommodates the winter weather, bringing light into the centre of the building for public activities. Henrik Bull's office building for Christopher Hannevig (1918) in Oslo has a sophisticated three-part classical façade with refined detailing (*see* Fig. 6.11).

In the 1920s Nordic architects travelled south and were inspired by the classically influenced vernacular churches and buildings of the Italian hill towns. The classical architecture of the Mediterranean created public spaces and buildings that provided both a humanizing and civilizing touch to the landscape; and Scandinavian architects desired to create buildings, spaces and architectural elements that brought such a touch to the rugged Nordic landscape. The

Fig. 2.8 Lars Sonck's striking Tampere Cathedral (1907) exemplifies romantic compositional sensibilities with its irregular massing, asymmetrical placing of forms and elements and use of rough stone construction. (Photo: Author).

Fig. 2.9 The *Jugendstil*-influenced Helsinki Central Railway Station (1914) by Eliel Saarinen signals the movement away from National Romanticism to a more refined, yet expressive, classical direction. (Photo: Author)

sketchbooks of Erik Gunnar Asplund, Erik Bryggman, Ragnar Östberg, Hilding Ekelund and Alvar Aalto, among others, are filled with drawings of this *architettura minore* – classically inspired, unpretentious, everyday Italian buildings.

The desire to use architecture as a civilizing agent within the Nordic landscape is articulated in Alvar Aalto's writings of the 1920s:

> There are many examples of pure harmonious, civilized landscapes in the world: one finds real gems in Italy and the South of France … Central Finland frequently reminds one of Tuscany, the homeland of towns built on hills, which should provide an indication of how classically beautiful our province could be if built up properly.[19]
>
> …
>
> Take for example, Ronninmäki Hill, which dominates the countryside around Jyväskylä. It would only need a white campanile near (not

at) the top for the whole area to acquire an aura of refinement … A real tower would make the whole landscape classical.[20]

The desire was to create architecture with simplified yet classical, graceful forms. Despite classical uniforms these buildings often contained numerous non-classical characteristics: floor plans incorporating asymmetrical arrangements that accommodated both functional necessities and the demands of site; the use of simply proportioned geometric forms with sparsely decorated stucco, brick and wood surfaces; and details that are often exaggerated or whimsical. Numerous public and civic buildings were executed in this style, as were many housing estates, private houses and industrial works. This speaks of an aesthetic democratization where homes for both wage earners and *nouveau riche* were dressed in classical simplicity. The Nordic Classicism of the 1920s was also bound to a new professional self-assurance which involved liberation from academic tradition as well as the stylistic eclecticism of the nineteenth century; hence the willingness to be more whimsical in expression.

Denmark

One of the first significant manifestations of this new classicism is seen in Carl Peterson's Art Museum (1915) (Fig. 2.10) in Fåborg which expresses a sense of clarity and timelessness, through a rich and extensive use of interior colour. Two important public and civic buildings in Copenhagen are Hack Kampmann's monumental and severe police headquarters

Fig. 2.10 The interior of Carl Peterson's classically referenced Fåborg Art Museum (1915) incorporates a rich and extensive use of colour, including the elaborate patterning of the floor mosaics. (Photo: Author)

(1921) and the historicist New Carlsberg Glyptotek (1906).

Several large housing projects were developed in Copenhagen: Povl Baumann's flats on Borups Allé (1916, with Ivar Bentsen) and housing complex at Struensegade (1920) and Kay Fisker's high-density Hornbaek House (1923). These complexes were quite large, multi-storeyed and formed around significant internal landscaped communal spaces. At the residential scale, refined classical works include Povl Baumann's villa for Aage Lund (1916), Poul Holsøe's own house (1917) and Holgar Jacobsen's own house (1925), all in Copenhagen.

Other exemplary projects are Kaj Gottlob and Anton Frederiksen's austere St Luke's Church (1926) in Aarhus; Edvard Thomsen's clear and rational Øregaard Secondary School (1924) in Hellerup, which is organized around a light-filled atrium, and his more expressionistic Søndermark Crematorium (1930) designed with Frits Schlegel; and Ivar Bentsen's simple, monumental Svinninge power station (1913).

Norway

One of the most comprehensive and integrated classical urban spaces of this period is the Torgallmenningen Square in Bergen (1922–29) by Finn Berner (Fig. 2.11). The square is formed by a series of simple cubic building, with a two-storey colonnade at plaza level and horizontal string coursing on the façades integrating the composition. It is interesting how this seeming anonymous classicism fosters a dignified urban architecture, much like the *architettura minore* of northern Italy captured in Nordic architects' sketchbooks. Berner also executed the refined Bergen Telegraph Building (1927) with Anton M. Kielland. The Haugesund Town Hall (1931) by Gudolf Blakstad and Herman Munthe-Kaas has an astonishing pink stucco upper volume surmounting a granite base. Colour was often used to activate the plain stucco surfaces throughout the Nordic countries.

Fig. 2.11 Finn Berner's Torgallmenningen Square (1929) in Bergen illustrates how the simplicity of 1920s Nordic Classicism can create a dignified urban architecture and public space using simple unadorned building forms and selective classical elements. (Photo: Author)

In Oslo, from single houses like the Frithjof Larsen residence (1925) by Lars Becker and Nicolai Beer's own house (1921), to Harald Hals's Ullevål Hageby (1915–22) and the Nordre and Søndre Åsen (1926) housing districts, classicism reigned. Lorentz Ring's Vigeland Museum (1925) has interiors inspired by Norwegian neoclassicism. The first redesign of Magnus Poulsson and Arnstein Arneberg's Oslo City Hall began in 1930, resulting in the composition that shaped the final design. While classical in its repose, there was a nascent modernism in the proposal.

Sweden

'Swedish Grace' was the term describing the classicism of the 1920s and Ivar Tengbom produced some of the most influential works of this period. In Stockholm, the Enskilda Bank (1915) with its rusticated ground floor, the School of Economics (1926) with its simple rhythmical façade composition, the iconic Concert Hall (1926) and the Matchstick Palace (1928) with its horseshoe-shaped courtyard all characterize the expressive range Tengbom achieved with this abstract classicism. The Concert Hall is a freestanding, monolithic blue cube penetrated by numerous small windows. The tall, slender colonnade with a delicate entablature animates Hötoget, the public square it fronts.

A sensitive classicism is characteristic of Erik Gunnar Asplund's early work. The Chapel (1920) at Stockholm's Woodland Cemetery appears like a forest hut with primitive roof and Doric portico, yet houses a sophisticated sky-lit domed interior. The façade of the Lister District Courthouse (1921) incorporates mannered, classical elements. The Skandia Cinema (1924) in Stockholm is a festive, dreamlike world: the auditorium recalls an outdoor space open to the starry night sky surrounded with canopied balconies. The internationally acclaimed Stockholm Public Library (1928) presents a radically simplified, elemental set of interlocking archetypal volumes: cube and cylinder (Fig. 2.12). The raised cylinder dominating the composition houses a clerestoried lending and reading room, while the interior spaces are excellently detailed throughout.

Other important works include Carl Bergsten's elegant Liljevalch Art Hall (1916) in Stockholm; Erik Lallerstedt's Stockholm University Law and Humanities Faculty (1926); Sigurd Lewerentz's Resurrection Chapel (1926) in the Woodland Cemetery; Ragnar Östberg's Maritime Museum (1934) in Stockholm and Crematorium (1928) in Helsingborg; Georg A. Nilsson's High School at Fridhemsplan (1927) in Stockholm and Gunnar Leche's Vaksala School (1927) in Uppsala. Cyrillus Johansson's Värmlands regional museum (1929) in Karlstad seamlessly combines Chinese elements with classical ones.

Fig. 2.12 The iconic Stockholm Public Library (1928) by Erik Gunnar Asplund is a radically simplified archetypal set of architectural volumes: the cube and the cylinder. The clerestoried cylinder holds the three-storey public reading room while the cube houses a variety of library activities. (Photo: By Holger.Ellgaard (Own work) [CC BY-SA 3.0 (http://creativecommons.org/licenses/by-sa/3.0)], via Wikimedia Commons)

The Götaplatsen (1917), an important urban complex in Gothenburg designed by Sigfrid Ericson, E. Torulf, A. Bjerke and R.O. Svensson, is the city's cultural hub. Composed around an open square housing Carl Milles's *Poseidon* (1931), each building is unique in its expression. The Gothenburg Museum of Art (1923) by Ericson has a solid refined yellow brick façade with an arched loggia; Carl Bergsten's Gothenburg City Theatre (1934) has idiosyncratic elements including caryatid figures; and the Gothenburg Concert Hall (1935) by Nils Einar Eriksson is modernist in form yet classical in repose.

Finland

When Finland was ceded to Russia in the Napoleonic settlement, the new Grand Duchy was brought into the nineteenth century socially, politically and, importantly, architecturally. From the provincial and vernacular architecture of Finland's rural past, as a result of Russian intervention, the country was abruptly propelled into the cosmopolitan world of neoclassicism. Carl Ludwig Engel's magnificent Senate Square (1818–40) came to represent the public architectural style of the new Grand Duchy, transforming the then small town of Helsinki. Moreover, Engel's influence is seen throughout Finland where his numerous neoclassical works brought a modernizing, civilizing and humanizing touch to the countryside.

With independence achieved in 1917, it is not surprising that Finnish architects embraced classicism. They felt connection with the Mediterranean would culturally improve the civic, architectural and planning milieu of the recently independent country in urban as well as rural locales. As Alvar Aalto stated, 'In towns, public buildings accentuate the lines of squares and street perspectives. In the country, their function is to accentuate the landscape.'[21]

Women began entering the architectural profession in Finland in the 1890s after attending the Polytechnic Institute in Helsinki. Numerous photographs from the Polytechnic's studios and classrooms in the 1890s show the important presence of women in the Institute. In 1890, Signe Hornberg was the first woman to receive an architectural degree.

Women made essential architectural contributions to the development of both National Romanticism and 1920s Nordic Classicism. Signe Hornberg, who worked for Lars Sonck after graduation, designed the Newlander apartment building (1892) in Pori and the façade of the Sepänkatu building (1897) in Helsinki, both

eclectic, historicist works. Signe Lagerborg-Stenius designed *Jugendstil*-inspired buildings for the Supervisory Board for Public Buildings, including the Children's Home (1895) and the Children's Shelter (1910) in Helsinki and the Ljungbo Sanatorium (1910) in Hanko.

During the National Romantic period, Wivi Lönn, an incredibly productive architect, produced the Finnish Girls School (1902), the Alexander School (1904), the Domestic Management School (1905), the Central Fire Station (1908) – a signature work – and the Business School, all in Tampere (1912).

The 1920s saw the construction of exemplary Nordic classic works

such as Elsi Borg's powerful, monumental Taulumäki Church (1928) in Jyväskylä (Fig. 2.13); Elsa Arokallio's military barracks (1922) in Kahava and the Lucina Hagman School (1926) in Helsinki; Eva Kuhlefelt-Ekelund's skilfully proportioned Private Swedish Girls' School (1929) in Helsinki; and Kerttu Rytkönen's private Salus Hospital (1929) in Helsinki. As an independent commission Aino Aalto executed the rural Villa Flora (1926) in Alajärvi.

The number of Finnish women entering the architectural profession at the beginning of the twentieth century was both remarkable and unique.[22] By 1930 about fifty women architects were at work in the country.

Fig. 2.13 Elsi Borg's Taulumäki Church (1928) in Jyväskylä is a powerful austere work revealing the abstract, yet somewhat playful, character of 1920s Nordic Classicism. (Photo: Tiia Monto [CC BY-SA 3.0 (http://creativecommons.org/licenses/by-sa/3.0)], via Wikimedia Commons)

In Helsinki, Martti Välikangas's unique Käpylä Garden City (1925) and Gunnar Taucher's block of flats on Mäkelänkatu (1926) were important housing projects. Hilding Ekelund executed two somewhat idiosyncratic works: the 'Taidehalli' or Art Hall (1927) and Töölö Church (1930). Three large and very significant urban works were P.E. Blomstedt's 'Liittopankki' Bank (1929) and the Finnish Savings Bank (1930), both influenced by the American architect Louis Sullivan, and Sigurd Frosterus's muscular masonry Stockmann's department store (1930).

The wife-and-husband team of Aino and Alvar Aalto began their career during this time and, along with Erik Bryggman, produced some of the most interesting works outside of Helsinki. Bryggman, whose classicism had a light Italianate touch, executed the block of flats on Brahenkatu (1924), the Cinema 'Olympia' (1926) and the 'Atrium' apartment block (1927), all in Turku.

Alvar and Aino Aalto produced the Palladian inspired Worker's Club in Jyväskylä (1924); the Civil Guards complex in Seinäjoki (1925); the Patriotic Association in Jyväskylä (1929); the Southwest Agricultural Association building (1929) in Turku; and the Italian vernacular-influenced Muurame Church (1929). Work for the Civil Guards and Patriotic Association produced a building type unique to Finland; they housed voluntary defence organizations formed after the civil war but later disbanded.

The crowning achievement of this period in Finland was J.S. Siren's monumental Parliament building (1930) in Helsinki. The rose-coloured granite tour de force provided the new nation with a 'national town hall', a work equivalent in standing to the Copenhagen, Stockholm and Oslo town halls.

Ready for Modernity

By the mid-1920s, when avant-garde architectural ideas from the Continent were beginning to travel north, Scandinavia had transformed into a region geared for architectural as well as social progress.

Both National Romanticism and the classicism of the 1920s were important to this transformation. Nordic self-assuredness came from a renewed sense of national identity and purpose on one hand and an evolution into modern, industrialized, urban and democratic societies on the other. Socially and politically the foundation for the development of the modern social welfare state had been laid. Architecturally, this resulted in new city halls, universities, schools, libraries, museums, cultural facilities and social services; all buildings for important democratic institutions. Buildings for communication and transportation – railway stations, telephone and telegraph offices and post offices – tied Nordic countries together by furthering the capacity of citizens to interact and connect with each other.

Beyond developing new building types for an emergent progressive society, Nordic architects provided potent and persuasive symbols that architecturally represented and celebrated these institutions. The convincing new urban town halls, national museums and cultural facilities and train stations and telephone facilities provided national, cultural and social identities for the citizens of the North. *Fin-de-siècle* National Romanticism produced an amazing array of significant emblematic civic works throughout Scandinavia. These works literally transformed the people's understanding of their heritages and place in the world. The Nordic Classicism of the 1920s sought to use architecture to help humanize and civilize the landscape and cityscapes of the North. In both urban and rural situations, architecture brought order by creating the public space of squares and streets while accentuating the country landscape.

The reductionist quality of 1920s Nordic Classicism also laid the foundation for the acceptance of the abstraction and rationality found in modernism in the late 1920s and early 1930s. Numerous younger architects practising classicism became quick converts to modernism: Erik Gunnar Asplund, Sigurd Lewerentz, Alvar and Aino Aalto, Erik Bryggman, Lars Becker, Arne Jacobsen and Carl Peterson, among others.

Chapter 3

MODERNISM ARRIVES IN SCANDINAVIA: NORDIC FUNCTIONALISM

THE ARCHITECTURAL DIRECTIONS THAT materialized in continental Europe following the First World War responded to the period's passionate and idealistically motivated desire to create fresh architectural themes and forms that could contribute to a liberated 'modern' society. The quest for a 'new' architecture occurred in Germany, France, Italy, the Netherlands and the Soviet Union in response to the modernizing of industrial society, rapid urbanization and the growth of Continental cities and the rebuilding of Europe after the destruction of the war.

Basic to the idea of a modern architecture was the notion that each age possessed its own authentic style, or *Zeitgeist*, that expressed the true tenor of the time or epoch. Architects felt that traditional forms were outdated in the new economic, social and political environment of an ever-industrializing world. Architects desired to be responsive to the new social conditions and conventions and to contemporary materials and construction techniques, while seeking fresh expressive and symbolic forms. The post-war setting was viewed as the time to create the new modern world and architects and artists sought to 'Make it new!' through their work (Figs 3.1 and 3.3).

Fig. 3.1 The Festival Square of the 1930 Stockholm Exhibition, with its constructivist advertising tower, the Functionalist Paradise Restaurant and exhibition pavilions by chief architects Erik Gunnar Asplund and Sigurd Lewerentz, promoted the image of a new modern world in architecture and design. (Photo: Courtesy of the Swedish Centre for Architecture and Design's collections, photographer: Nikolaj Alsterdal)

Fig. 3.2 The Luma Lightbulb Factory (1930) in Stockholm, by Artur von Schmalensee and Eskil Sundahl, is emblematic of Functionalism's organizational strategies and machine aesthetics, with its concrete frame construction, horizontal ribbon windows, cantilevered elements and industrial detailing. (Photo: By Holger Ellgaard (Own work) [CC BY-SA 3.0 (http://creativecommons.org/licenses/by-sa/3.0)], via Wikimedia Commons)

Le Corbusier's Purism in France, van Doesberg's and Rietveld's *De Stijl* in the Netherlands, Futurism in Italy, constructivism in the Soviet Union and the Bauhaus School in Germany under Walter Gropius and Mies van der Rohe were representative of the avant-garde artistic and architectural directions. Common among these was the desire to create an architectural expression representing contemporary cultural forces such as revolutionary social change, speed and dynamism coupled with an aggressive adulation of the machine and the use of industrial processes and serial production techniques for buildings and everyday consumer products. Architects wanted to capture the equivalent expressive power of ships, trains, planes and automobiles as these were serially produced or built by industrial processes. What emerged was an expression combining formal abstraction with machine imagery that was realized using white cubic volumes, flat roofs, horizontal ribbon windows and minimalistic industrial- or nautical-inspired detailing. That buildings began looking like machines was no accident.

Scandinavian architects' awareness of the new ideas emerging from the Continent began in the mid-1920s,

as Nordic architectural journals began publishing the work of French, German, Dutch and Russian avant-garde architects. Scandinavian architects, who at the time were practising the austere Nordic Classicism, were particularly open to currents from the outside. Nordic architects attended pivotal architectural exhibitions and congresses promoting the new architecture on the Continent, as well as visiting modernism's early seminal works. Moreover, they regularly published reviews of the contemporaneous work that appeared in both professional and popular publications. Theoretical and polemical discussions resulted from the lectures of Le Corbusier and Walter Gropius in the North. This first-hand knowledge of contemporary avant-garde buildings and ideas was instrumental in the promulgation of '*Funktionalism*' or 'Functionalism', as modernism was called in Scandinavia.

As Functionalism took root in Scandinavia, it was realized in houses and housing projects, as well as civic, religious and cultural buildings, commercial structures and educational and health-care facilities, along with newer building types such as cinemas, petroleum stations, factories and labour unions' and worker associations' headquarters (Figs 3.2 and 3.7).

Architecture for leisure activities promoting sports and physical health became increasingly popular in the North, as seen in the growth of sports facilities, public baths and bathing resorts.

What characterized these works was an organizational strategy that relied on the expression of a buildings programme articulated as discrete spaces, volumes and forms and realized through abstract cubic planar surfaces rendered in a continuous material – most often stucco; flat roofs often with roof terraces and gardens; large amounts of glazing frequently composed as horizontal ribbon windows; and the use of industrial (often nautically inspired) detailing and expression. In addition, architects desired that their buildings appear weightless, so steel and concrete frame construction was often used to support the bulk of the building above a glazed or open ground floor. By having the upper portion of the building appear to be held up by glazing or slim columns, a sense of weightlessness, timelessness and modernity was imbued to the structure through the use of the latest construction techniques

Functionalism emphasized the expectations of a better world realized through the assistance of modern technology and rational planning. Functionalist architecture postulated a higher standard of living, which would produce generally healthier housing; well-lit, airy, with hygienic services and placed in open green or park-like settings. The social aspect of Functionalism promoted democratic ideals which reinforced the role of the then emerging Nordic welfare states and their focus on a sense of equality and care.

Numerous exhibitions promoting modern architecture and living occurred during the late 1920s and early 1930s in Scandinavia, which contributed significantly to the promulgation and acceptance of Nordic Functionalism (*see* Figs 3.1, 3.3 and 3.5) (*see* 'The House of the Future'). The architecture of these exhibitions, while temporary, embraced the machine aesthetics and industrialized construction processes of modernism and provided the participants with a powerful sense of a new modern world. Common

were examples of new housing prototypes informing the viewer of how one would live in the future and that included the new serially produced products and objects that would equip the house: furniture, labour-saving appliances, lighting fixtures, eating utensils, fabrics and more. These exhibitions offered the Nordic citizen a first-hand picture of the future of modern living and its concomitant qualities.

Denmark

While Norwegian architect Edvard Heiberg's own house of 1924, outside Copenhagen, was the earliest modern work in Scandinavia, the 1929 'House of the Future Exhibition' held in Copenhagen brought modernism to Denmark (*see* 'The House of the Future'). Arne Jacobsen's 'House of the Future', designed with Flemming Lassen, established them as progressive modern architects. Jacobsen had travelled to France and Germany in the mid-1920s and his work immediately embraced Continental architectural concepts. Having executed several modern houses in Copenhagen's suburbs, he created a series of buildings in the suburb of Klampenborg that revealed his sophistication in assimilating ideas from the Bauhaus and other Continental sources. In 1932 Jacobsen executed the popular Bellavista Sea Bath complex, which included lifeguard towers, kiosks and changing cabins. Next, across from the bath complex is the Bellavista housing estate (1934) (Fig. 3.4), the Bellevue theatre and restaurant complex (1936) and the nearby Texaco petrol station (1938). Demonstrating his ability to use modern principles in designing new building types, the theatre originally featured an interior canvas covering that could slide back on warm summer evenings to reveal the starry night sky. In the Stelling Building (1937) in Copenhagen, Jacobsen capitalizes on Functionalism's desire to create the image of a weightless building through creating a two-storey glazed ground level appearing to support the heavier office floors above. Here modernity meets a sense of classical repose.

Le Corbusier's iconic Villa Savoy (1929) was referred to as a 'machine for living'. The house floated above the ground, raised on thin concrete columns called *pilotis*. The planar white surfaces, horizontal ribbon windows, nautical detailing and bridge-like roof terrace elicit an industrial ship-like image. It appears a machine free of the static contact with the ground found in the architecture of the past; a ship moving powerfully over an open, airy, healthy sea of green grass.

Arne Jacobsen and Flemming Lassen's 'House of the Future' (1929) (Fig. 3.3) not only captures this machine aesthetic through its taut stucco surfaces, horizontal strip windows and ship rail detailing, but expresses the mobility and dynamism of modernity through incorporation of an automobile, speed boat and heli-plane into the design. Located in the forest next to a waterway, the house could be rotated to follow the sun during the day. The kitchen included the most recent labour-saving devices, providing the woman of the house with freedom to engage fully in an active modern urban lifestyle, including leisure time to sun-bathe on the roof terrace. Few other works, in Scandinavia or the Continent, capture the essence of the new modern house as well as this design and at the same time appear a kind of Functionalist fantasy.

Fig. 3.3 Arne Jacobsen and Flemming Lassen's 'House of the Future' (1929) was designed for the 'House of the Future' Exhibition in Copenhagen and captures the spirit and dynamics of a new modern world with its accommodation of the car, heli-plane and boat. (Photo: Courtesy of the Danish National Art Library, Collection of Architectural Drawings)

In the Broadcast Building in Copenhagen (1935), Vilhelm Lauritzen merges the development of a new building type lacking historical precedent with modern architecture's preference for using elemental forms to express the building programme. The complex consists of elements which outwardly express their inner function. There are the four- and five-storey office wings incorporating horizontal window bands and a canopied main entrance. Behind this is a more solid wing housing the performance

and broadcast studios of the complex. The trapezoid concert hall grows out of these two parts and expresses itself through its bold curving roof form with an attached articulated entrance and foyer element. A roof garden completes the composition. Each element distinctly expresses its function in both space and form, while the building is constructed of a singular material – yellow masonry units. Lauritzen's design for the air terminal in the Copenhagen suburb of Kastrup (1939) captures Functionalism's machine imagery, featuring a large open hall with a dramatic undulating perforated wood fibreboard ceiling.

Mogens Lassen, inspired by the work of Le Corbusier, demonstrated his assimilation of Corbusian concepts in the Ishøj house (1934), his own house (1935) and three villas (1939) on Sølystvej (numbers 5, 7 and 11) in Copenhagen's Klampenborg suburb. Lassen stated that Functionalism '… is the language which best permits a free and artistic formulation of the tasks.'[23] This was demonstrated in his house designs as well as in his expressive five-storey Systems House (1937), an apartment complex in Ordrup.

Poul Henningsen, while educated as an architect, is known for his progressive polemical left-wing writings on Danish culture as editor of the *Kritisk Revy* in the late 1920s, but especially for the design of the iconic 'PH-lamp' (1925). The lamp was one of the most popular emblems of modern design and used by numerous architects of the period in their buildings. It is still a popular light fixture today.

Other exemplary Functionalist works in Denmark included: Poul Holsøe's circular concrete Brønshøj Water Tower (1930), Frits Schlegel's *Overformynderiet* or Public Trustees' Office (1930) and the evocative Hotel Astoria (1935) by Ole Falkentorp, all in Copenhagen. Kaj Gottlob's 'School by the Sound' (1938) in Copenhagen, designed for children with health problems, embraces modernism's social programme through its open-air courtyard design and exterior glazing that captured light and fresh air and provided immediate contact with the outside. Edvard Thomsen's apartment complex (1939) at H.C. Ørsteds Vej 54 in the Copenhagen suburb of Frederiksberg creatively uses glass block in its concrete structural frame. Also in Frederiksberg are Frits Schlegel and Magnus Stephensen's sculpturally expressive mixed-use Old King's Farm (1939) and Frederiksberg Farm (1940) complexes.

Fig. 3.5 Erik Gunnar Asplund's Paradise Restaurant for the 1930 Stockholm Exhibition illustrates the lightness of construction and timelessness of form in the Exhibition's major buildings and pavilions. The multi-storeyed restaurant had sleek nautical detailing and playful banners on the interior. (Photo: (Paradise rest/1930 by okänt (Husen på Malmarna) [Public domain], via Wikimedia Commons)

Sweden

The 1930 Stockholm Exhibition (Figs 3.1 and 3.5), by chief architects Erik Gunnar Asplund and Sigurd Lewerentz, was not only a truly seminal work, it firmly established Functionalism as the dominant architectural style in Sweden. The exhibition was a call for acknowledging rationality, efficiency, standardization and mass production as necessary for fostering cultural change. It was an effort to persuade Swedish citizens of the benefits of a modern lifestyle and while the buildings were temporary, the ideas embedded in them continued to influence and shape Swedish architecture and product design for years.

The buildings of the exhibition were composed of glass, steel-framed structures and thin panelling that achieved a lightness that made them seem ageless. The Paradise Restaurant (Fig. 3.5) and the entry pavilion best exemplify the light, airy, transparent, colourful and taut nautical quality of the exhibition buildings. The idiosyncratic advertising tower, the major vertical accent within the overall plan of the

fair, had an exaggerated and playful structural quality, with constructivist-inspired graphics for the advertising (*see* Fig. 3.1). There were examples of numerous modern house designs by Sweden's best-known architects, as well as pavilions showcasing the new industrially produced products for use in the home and office. For the visitor a new world was presented!

Of the architects and writers involved in the Stockholm Exhibition, Sven Markelius, Uno Åhrén, Erik Gunnar Asplund, Eskil Sundahl, Wolter Gahn and Gregor Paulsson produced the document *acceptera* (*accept*) in 1931. Considered the manifesto of Nordic Functionalism, the text asserts that only the new architecture could adequately address the needs of the time. Functionalism prevailed in the North because its message also suited the requirements of the emerging welfare state.

While the exhibition celebrated and institutionalized Swedish modernism, among the first public buildings to embrace Functionalism was Sven Markelius's Helsingborg Concert Hall (1932) (Fig. 3.6). Markelius reworked his original winning 1926

Fig. 3.6 Demonstrative of Functionalism's organizational strategy, Sven Markelius's Concert Hall (1932) in Helsingborg is composed of white elemental forms volumetrically expressing each particular programmatic function: the round entry and ticket office, the linear promenade, vertical staircases and the cubic concert hall. (Photo: (By Jsdo1980 (Own work) [GFDL (http://www.gnu.org/copyleft/fdl. html) or CC BY 3.0 (http://creativecommons.org/licenses/by/3.0)], via Wikimedia Commons)

competition entry after visiting the 1927 Weissen-hoffsiedlung Housing Exhibition in Stuttgart and the Bauhaus School (1926) in Dessau in 1927. It is a work executed in white concrete with elemental forms that volumetrically expresses each particular programmatic function in the complex: entry and ticket office, promenade and foyer and concert hall. Works by Markelius in Stockholm include the Kvarteret Berget apartment building (1929), the Gräset housing complex (1930), the residence hall at the Stockholm Technical College (1930, with Uno Åhrén), his own house (1931) and the Collective House apartment complex (1936). These buildings further demonstrate his exemplary mastery and execution of modern design concepts, materiality and industrialized detailing.

In addition to his instrumental role in realizing the Stockholm Exhibition, Asplund designed the Bredenberg department store (1936) and the State Bacteriological Laboratories (1937), both in Stockholm. The upper storeys of the department store,

located on a narrow downtown site, appear to float above the glass entry level. The façade is articulated with horizontal ribbon windows and accentuated by modern neon signage (now removed). The State Laboratories are highlighted by their white machine-like interiors. Lewerentz's mastery of Functionalism was seen not only in the works he executed for the Stockholm Exhibition, but in his sophisticated use of the language used in the office building for Philips AB (1930) and the Social Security Administration building (1932), both in Stockholm, and the Cemetery Chapel (1932) in Enköping.

Hakon Ahlberg's Hjorthagen housing complex (1937) in suburban Stockholm was the first in Sweden to use serially produced construction products and techniques to build a large-scale housing project. The influence of the Stockholm Exhibition can be seen in Södra Ängby, a residential area in western Stockholm, blending Functionalism with British-inspired garden-city ideals. Built between 1933 and 1940 and encompassing more than 500 buildings, it remains the largest coherent ensemble of individual villas in Sweden designed with Functionalist principles: white cubic volumes, flat roofs, generous windows, balconies and nautical-inspired detailing. Edvin Engström designed the great majority of the villas, which are on fenceless plots within the continuous forested site.

Functionalist works in Stockholm and its suburbs included Olof Thunström's terraced house complex for mill workers (1930); the uncompromisingly modernist Hotel Eden (1930) by Björn Hedvall with continuous horizontal windows on all floors; and Ivar Tengbom's ribbon-windowed concrete frame Esselte publishing house (1934) which was covered with neon signage at the time. Paul Hedqvist executed the programmatically expressed Lovöns water purification plant (1930), Bromma Airport (1936) and St Erik's School (1939) with its distinctive glass-cylinder exterior staircase. In addition there is the sophisticated and rational Luma Lightbulb Factory (1930) (*see* Fig. 3.2) by Artur von Schmalensee and Eskil Sundahl; Muaritz Dahlberg and Herbert Kockum's mixed-use Påhlman Business Institute (1930); and Uno Åhrén's Flamman cinema (1930). Nils Ahrbom and Helge Zimdahl's elementally composed Sveaplan High School for Girls (1936), with well-proportioned façades and expressive volumes, and the dramatic Katrina lift and office complex for the Cooperative Union and Wholesale Society by Eskil Sundahl and Olof Thunström (1936) are exemplars of Functionalism. Paul Hedqvist also designed the impressive swimming baths (1933) in Eskilstuna with its glazed pool area.

Norway

In 1925, Norwegian Lars Becker wrote in *Byggekunst*, 'We shall create an architecture in contact with the times we live in, suited to the materials with which we build. We shall abandon concealment and all exterior frippery, function shall decide form. Plan and façade should be one.'[24] In advocating architecture based upon purpose and structural honesty,

Becker's rational and austere Skansen Restaurant (1927, demolished in 1979) in Oslo was the first relatively large Functionalist building in Scandinavia, yet retained some classicist qualities. His Restaurant Ekeberg (1929) in Oslo with its open plan, clear construction and austere horizontal planar surfaces rendered in stucco is a true Functionalist work. In 1928, Becker designed the Horngården building for downtown Oslo – the city's tallest at the time. It was to be thirteen storeys with a continuous glass façade and rounded corners, but opposition to the progressive nature of this design resulted in a more conservative eight-storey building.

Ove Bang was considered the most important exponent of Functionalism in Norway, as he was able to unify Continental influences with local traditions, developing a personal style that was straightforward and powerful. The Villa Ditlev-Simonsen (1937) is a very sophisticated work, every bit as erudite as Le Corbusier's contemporaneous houses. The Workers Association Community Building (1939) (Fig. 3.7) in Oslo, Bang's most important work, has a clear structural system which provides coherence to a varied and expressive façade. Here, modernism's interest in expressing programmatic function is articulated through the compositions of the façades. Bang died during the war, unfortunately for the development of Norwegian modernism.

Arne Korsmo designed Oslo's first Functionalist houses and housing developments; they incorporated open site planning and white cubic building forms with flat roofs and large window surfaces. Exemplary works included the Havna housing development (1932), the Damman House (1932, with Sverre Aasland), the Hansen House (1935), the Benjamin House (1935), the Heyerdahl House (1936) and the Villa Stenersen (1939) (Fig. 3.8), all located in Oslo, in addition to the Riise House (1935) in Hamar. At the Villa Stenersen, the glazing indicates the nature of the spaces behind; public spaces with clear glazing, semi-public behind the glass block and private spaces behind the walls with smaller punched window openings. The mid-western American grain elevator was

Fig. 3.7 In Ove Bang's Workers Association Community building (1939) in Oslo, the façade expresses the building's different programmatic functions – cinema, restaurant and ground-level commercial, offices and dormitory units and the upper-level outdoor terrace – all within a regulated column grid. (Photo: By Kjetil Ree Architect: Ove Bang (Own work) [CC BY-SA 2.5-2.0-1.0 (http://creativecommons.org/licenses/by-sa/2.5-2.0-1.0)], via Wikimedia Commons)

Fig. 3.8 The Villa Stenersen (1939) in Oslo, by Arne Korsmo, exemplifies his use of Functionalist cubic building forms with flat roof and large glazing surfaces including glass block. (Photo: By John Lord from Edinburgh, Scotland (Villa Stenersen) [CC BY 2.0 (http://creativecommons.org/licenses/by/2.0)], via Wikimedia Commons)

an emblematic design precedent for modern architects and Korsmo's Grain Store (1936) in Kristiansand captures the essence of this iconic form.

In Bergen, Leif Grung, a highly productive and outspoken Functionalist, designed several exceptional modern works: the refined Villa Lau-Eide (1934), the mixed-use Blaauwgården office and storehouse (1936), the flowing sophisticated Kalmarhuset housing block

(1936) and the Fortunen apartment block (1938). Also in Bergen is the Kunsthall (1935) by Ole Landmark and the Bauhaus-inspired Sundt department store (1938) on Torgallmenningen Square by Per Grieg (Fig. 3.9). Viewed from the square, Sundt's glazed ground-floor level, horizontal ribbon windows, large vertical glazed area, white stucco surfaces and signage all speak Functionalism's aesthetic language.

Fig. 3.9 Per Grieg's Sundt department store (1938) in Bergen's Torgallmenningen Square was inspired by Walter Gropius's Bauhaus School (1926) in Dessau, Germany. (Photo: By Odd Roar Aalborg (Own work) [CC BY-SA 3.0 no (http://creativecommons.org/licenses/by-sa/3.0/no/deed.en)], via Wikimedia Commons)

Exemplary Functionalist works in Oslo include: Blakstad and Munthe-Kaas's Artist's House (1930) and their horizontal banded glass and panel Odd Fellows Building (1934); Frithjof Reppen's Weissenhoffsiedlung-inspired Professor Dahls Gate housing complex (1932); Eyvind Moestue and Ole Lind Schistad's impressive Engineers' Association building (1930) and their expressive and playful Ingierstrand open-air bathing resort (1934); and A.H. Bjercke and G. Eliassen's Restaurant Dronningen (1931). The circular Dobloug store (1933) by Rudolf Emanuel Jacobsen is based on the plans by German architect Erich Mendelsohn. Two housing complexes in Oslo express Functionalism's social programming: Ragnar Nilsen's Drammensveien 116B (1936) and Ree & Buch's Gabels Gate 46 (1938). Georg Fredrik Fasting designed a marvellous modernist telephone booth (1932); examples can still be seen around Oslo.

Finland

The Turku 700th Anniversary Fair and Exposition (1929), by Erik Bryggman and Alvar and Aino Aalto, introduced Functionalism to Finland through its open site planning, use of standardized building elements, modern graphics inspired by the Bauhaus and Russian Constructivism and machine-like imagery. While both Bryggman and the Aaltos were leaders in the development of Finnish modernism, it was the Aaltos who achieved an international reputation during the 1930s.

Alvar and Aino Aalto's *Turun Sanomat* building in Turku (1929) was the first Nordic work to incorporate Le Corbusier's 'Five Points for a New Architecture' into the design: the free plan, the free façade with horizontal ribbon windows, a roof terrace, the use of *pilotis* and concrete construction. Other significant Functionalist works by the Aaltos included the Standard Apartment block in Turku (1929), the

Fig. 3.10 The Tuberculosis Sanatorium (1933) in Paimio, by Alvar and Aino Aalto, is a superb example of Functionalism's ordering sensibilities and expression of its social programmes. (Photo: Author)

Tuberculosis Sanatorium at Paimio (1933) (Fig. 3.10) (*see* 'The Paimio Sanatorium') and the factory buildings and housing developments for the Sunila pulp mill complex (1935) in Kotka. The Sunila complex mixed work and living, exemplifying comprehensive modern planning principles and concepts: here one walked to work through the verdant forest and experienced the health-giving properties of the sun, fresh air and nature.

The sophistication of the Aaltos' work was, in part, due to their travels and connections with numerous Continental practitioners. As Finnish architect Hilding Ekelund wryly noted:

> With the same ardent enthusiasm as the academics of the 1880s drew Roman baroque portals, Gothic pinnacles, etc. in their sketchbooks for use in their architectural practice, Alvar Aalto noses out new, rational technical details from all over Europe which he then makes use of and transforms with considerable skill.[25]

Erik Bryggman's Finnish Pavilion for the 1930 Antwerp World's Fair combined modernist elemental forms with plywood sheathing to celebrate Finland's major industry. His Åbo Academy Library extension (1935) and Vierumäki Sports Institute (1936) are solid Functionalist works composed of white cubic forms expressing their programmes and articulated with horizontal ribbon windows. Other examples of his work in and around Turku at this time include the Parainen funeral chapel (1930) and several Functionalist villas.

P.E. (Pauli) Blomstedt, who passed away in 1935 at the age of 35, was a progressive Functionalist, as witnessed in his sophisticated use of modernist organizational principles and detail qualities and active embrace of its social programmes. This can be seen in his nautically influenced competition entry for the Kotka Town Hall (1931) and the urbane and refined Kotka Savings Bank (1935). He co-designed the impressive Hotel Pohjanhovi (1936) in Rovaniemi in concert with his wife, the architect Märta Blomstedt, but this was destroyed in the Russo-Finnish War. His final work, the small church in rural Kannonkoski (1938), was completed by his wife. Märta Blomstedt demonstrated her independent design capacities in the impressive Aulanko Hotel in Hämeenlinna (1938, with Matti Lampén).

Finland had an active Functionalist community, especially in Helsinki: Oiva Kallio's Pohja Insurance Company building (1930) emphasizes a strong horizontal strip-window composition; Kokko, Revell and Riihimäki's sleekly modern Glass Palace (1936) (*see* Fig. 7.9) housed the Bio-Rex cinema, a restaurant and provided a lively urban form elegantly shielding the city bus station behind it; while female architect

Martta Martikainen-Ypyä produced one of the finest works of the period, the barracks of the Vehicle Battalion (1935) – a work encapsulating modernism's desire to express efficiency and power. Aarne Hytönen and Risto-Veikkoa Luukkonen's expansive sports hall (1935) and Olavi Sortta's white nine-storey elementally composed Tilkka Hospital (1936) are also exemplary works. Yrjö Lindegren and Toivo Jäntti's Olympic Stadium (1938) (Fig. 3.11) became a national symbol of modern Finland. Executed originally for the 1940 Olympics, but postponed due to the war, the current wooden upper storey was modified to add more seats for the 1952 Olympic Games. Also built for the 1940 Olympics was Hilding Ekelund's elegant concrete velodrome (1940).

Erkki Huttunen executed a number of important works including the austere Kotka City Hall (1934), the expressive parish church in Nakkila (1937) and the SOK's office building and warehouse complex (1940) in Oulu. Bertel Strömmer's Sanatorium (1939)

Fig. 3.11 The 72-metre (235-foot) tower dominates Yrjö Lindegren and Toivo Jäntti's Olympic Stadium (1938) in Helsinki. Today the tower offers spectacular views of Helsinki (see Fig. 1.5). (Photo: Krysta Mae Dimick)

in Tammerfors captures modernism's austere expression, as does Viljo Revell's office building (1939) in Vasa.

During this period the city of Viipuri (now Vyborg, Russia) had important Functionalist works, including Erkki Huttunen's Hankkija office and warehouse (1932) and several works by Uno Ullberg: his elegant Viipuri Art Museum and Drawing School (1930, now the Hermitage-Vyborg Centre) with its courtyard overlooking the Baltic, the ribbon-windowed Panttilaitos office building (1934) and the elementally organized maternity hospital (1937). Ullberg executed several other health-care facilities in white Functionalist expression: the Kontinkangas hospital (1938) in Oulu, the Länsi-Pohja central hospital (1938) in Kimi and the Nursing Department building (1940) at the University of Helsinki.

There was an important difference between Continental modernism's social goals and the more humanistic ones that were forming in the North. Le Corbusier defined the aim of his basic planning principles as a recovery of 'elemental joys: sun, air and greenery',[26] joys lost in the nineteenth-century industrial city. His planning projects, which are characterized by high-rise housing blocks and highways set in green park-like settings, were intended to transform the Southern industrial city by creating a healthier and happier new urban world.

But the North is not the Mediterranean; it is a harsher, forested and rocky landscape set among rivers and lakes. Nordic Functionalist buildings were not machines in the garden or park as modernist works were in the South; they were machines in the forest and the forest can be an over-powering force. While assuming the mantle of modernism, Scandinavian architects, as seen in the next chapter, responded to a romantic cultural undercurrent that made contact and immediacy with nature important. While architects on the Continent tried to replace the nineteenth-century industrial city with an open green park-like tabula rasa, the architects of the North focused on re-establishing the link between humans and nature.

Alvar and Aino Aalto's Paimio Sanatorium (see Fig. 3.10) placed them at the forefront of important modern architects for two reasons. First, it is a superb example of Functionalism's use of programme to order and articulate a complex building. Second, it presented a potent realization of the social programmes that modern architecture promised – a healthy new world of sun, space and greenery as expressed by Le Corbusier. The physical presence of sun, green space and fresh air was sought in building designs because modern architects were convinced they promoted good health and well-being. And for the welfare state, the sanatorium exemplified the modern progressive health-care facility.

When examining the plan and form of the sanatorium, one observes that each of the programmatic elements of the building – the entry and circulation area, the patient wing, the sunning terraces, the communal and social areas, the service and support areas and garage – has a unique shape and separate form within the composition. The placement is not haphazard: the patient rooms and sunning terrace respond to solar orientation, breezes and forest views; and the communal and social wing, entry and patient wing create an open and accepting arrival space. The window configurations further articulate the function served: large glazed openings for the communal and social area; punched, large operable openings for the patient wing; and horizontal ribbon windows for the corridor and circulation areas.

The development of the sanatorium's interiors and furniture were important to the Aaltos, for no detail escaped their attention. From the specially designed windows, heating elements and sinks in the patients' rooms, through the door pulls and stair balustrades, down to the colours chosen for the various surfaces throughout the complex – all was thoughtfully considered and designed. They were also responsible for the furniture, designing the iconic 'Paimio' chair (see Fig. 4.10) that was used as a lounge chair by the patients (see 'Small Rehearsals of Form: Alvar and Aino Aalto's Applied Designs').

As a building type, the tuberculosis sanatorium became a most convincing public symbol of the new architecture. The actual medical treatment then recommended for tuberculosis – exposing patients throughout the day to lots of sunlight and fresh air – coincided exactly with the cultural metaphor of good health so central to the philosophy of modern architecture. Upon completion of such a prominent example of the new social architecture as the sanatorium at Paimio, the Aaltos emerged as major architects of the day.

Socially, with the advent and acceptance of Functionalism, there was a turn towards rational planning and functionality. It was the social implications of the architectural language which also gained a foothold in the Nordic cultural climate, which was sensitive to the questions of welfare and individual social improvement. The construction of appropriate modern houses and housing estates, daycare centres, hospitals and other building types enhancing social services, coupled with the design of functional furniture and household goods, became synonymous with the creation of social programmes promoting elderly care, child welfare, gender equality and education for the working class. Architecture, modern architecture, became inextricably part of the emerging modern Scandinavian social welfare state. Modernity in all its forms was enthusiastically embraced as the Nordic way.

Chapter 4

PLACE AND TRADITION MODIFY FUNCTIONALISM: A CRITIQUE

ALTHOUGH SCANDINAVIAN ARCHITECTS embraced Functionalism by the mid-thirties, almost immediately a number of individuals began questioning its basic precepts. Concerns regarding materiality and weathering were criticisms initially brought to bear on Functionalist works. As modernist buildings appeared in Scandinavia and the forces of nature and the impact of climate began to act upon them, architects questioned the advisability of using Mediterranean-inspired building forms and materials in the harsh northern environment. The Danish architect Esbjorn Hirt observed that Functionalism's 'unprotected white surfaces and flat roofs were unsuitable in our climate with its constant alternation between wet and dry and frost and thaw'.[27]

Architects and critics called for architecture less rigidly mechanistic and a reconsideration of such ideas as the role of history, monumentality and ornament in architecture. They further asked for an architecture that could tap the full range of human experiences and emotions. From a Continental perspective, ideas about modernism changed as dark clouds gathered over Europe. With the emergence and growth of repressive national states – Nazi Germany, fascist Italy and the communist Soviet Union – optimism was swept away and the development of modern art and architecture was suppressed and curtailed.

To modify Functionalism's abstract forms and limited material palette, architects incorporated more traditional forms, materials and window openings. This was a conscious attempt, as Hirt notes, 'to unite the modern demand for rational, unsymmetrical, "free" planning with the desire for a building profile suitable for the Danish climate'.[28] Traditional norms modified Functionalist aesthetics, providing more corporeal substance and regional character to the work. Interestingly, Le Corbusier's architecture had undergone a transformation during the late 1920s and early 1930s, influenced by vernacular cultures.

The response by Nordic architects assumed one of two directions: the first sought to modify Functionalism's focus on universal technique by using regional norms of expression and craft. Works by Arne Jacobsen, Frits Schegel, Kay Fisker, C.F. Møller, Flemming Lassen, Erik Møller and Erik Bryggman, among others, exemplify this direction. The second, seen in the work of Erik Gunnar Asplund and Alvar and Aino Aalto, resulted in reasserting the primacy of place, both physically and culturally, and employing the full gamut of sensory and tactile experiences that architecture can convey to an individual.

A common set of design strategies was generally employed throughout Scandinavia to modify Functionalism. Green park-like or forested environs were preferred as building sites so buildings could maintain their object quality. Designers integrated modernist open planning and elemental volumetrics with traditional building shapes and pitched-roof profiles. At the same time, overhangs were excluded from roof forms in a desire to maintain a taut, though sloped profile. Buildings often appeared more firmly rooted to the earth rather than uplifted on columns or *pilotis*. The resulting simplicity of form, coupled with the asymmetrical arrangement of elements and picturesque settings, often imbued the buildings with a quiet dignity and presence (Figs 4.1 and 4.2).

Fig. 4.1 The Resurrection Chapel (1940) in Turku, by Erik Bryggman, demonstrates the influence of traditional forms modifying modernist white austere surfaces; a simple stucco form with sloped roof is complemented by a stone wall, a traditional loggia with tile columns and planting. (Photo: Author)

Local materials supplanted the abstract, ephemeral character of Functionalist surfaces rendered in stucco. Satisfying this desire for increased corporeality and tactility, brick, tile, stone and wood wall cladding replaced stucco, while sloped roofs were finished with tile, shingles and metal. Often a single material dominated the execution of the building or complex, providing a uniform texture and colour. Although concrete or steel frames were employed in large buildings, many architects returned to traditional masonry and wood construction systems for more modest works. Simply proportioned punched window openings often replaced the modern horizontal ribbon window. While appearing a more traditional window type, the scale and proportions of the aperture, given the function or activity behind it, were enlarged and organized in a composition beyond the sizes usually governed by tradition.

While skylights had been used in many Scandinavian buildings since the late nineteenth century, during this period we see architects creating significant interior spaces that were generously lit (*see* Figs 4.4 and 4.7). Skylights became a more common way to light interior space, especially public and civic spaces, and a great variety of architectural forms were developed to link these rooms with the sky. This resulted in architects making more extensive use of openings in the ceiling and of clerestories in the upper walls to bring in the desired light, ensuring that the ever-changing light from the Nordic sky animated important interior spaces.

Throughout Scandinavia a number of representative works demonstrate these design tactics. In Denmark, Kay Fisker, Povl Stegmann and C.F. Møller's Aarhus University (1931–46) truly exemplifies this strategy of simplicity and clarity (Fig. 4.2). The architects married some of the best aspects of Functionalism with good Danish tradition in both form and materials. Set in a green, rolling, park-like setting with a small lake at its centre, the simple yellow brick volumes with taut pitched roofs display a consistency of building form and expression that binds the entire complex together. Punched window openings of various sizes and shapes articulate the different

Fig. 4.2 Rising above its park-like setting, the yellow brick architecture of Kay Fisker, Povl Stegmann and C.F. Møller's Aarhus University (1946) modifies Functionalist austerity through using regional materials and traditional sloped-roof building forms. The main building, with its large expressed *aula* or auditorium, is executed in a single material which provides a sense of dignity, solidity and calmness to the work. (Photo: Author)

functions within the individual buildings. Of particular note is the main building with its large public *aula* or auditorium space, the natural history museum and the chemistry, physics and anatomy building. These works demonstrate how variety and diversity can be achieved through using a very limited palette of materials and elements; a richness developed around the use of a single material, building placement on the site, recurring forms within the complex, well-studied building proportions and skilful crafting of the window openings and patterning.

Contrasting the Aarhus complex, Flemming Lassen and Erik Møller's Nyborg Public Library (1939) is a modest, more subtle work. The two simple taut red brick sloped roofed volumes are linked with a glass entry. The buildings are angled to engage their site, a peninsula in the river between Nyborg Castle and the town market. The sky-lit wood-panelled interior provides a warmth and clarity to the reading spaces. Like the Aarhus complex the library achieves great experiential qualities through a restrained material palette, subtle proportions and well-considered use of building elements. The Gladsaxes Town Hall (1937) by Vilhelm Lauritzen uses red brick cladding to soften and localize the rational, systematic floor plan. Inspired by the work of French architect Auguste Perret, Frits Schlegel designed the elegant and expressive concrete Mariebjerg Crematorium (1937) in Gentofte, with its custom-made blocks, special glazing in the façades and a vine-shrouded pergola softening the concrete surfaces.

Two housing complexes in Copenhagen by Kay Fisker and C.F. Møller show tactile modifications to modernist principles. The earlier complex at Vodroffsvej 2, Strygejernet (1929) in the Frederiksberg suburb has floor levels articulated with alternating red and yellow brick coursing; maintaining modernism's preference for horizontal emphasis, yet adding tactility and colour to the composition. The fenestration, while forming continuous horizontal bands, has articulated frames that eschew sleek machine imagery. The Vestorsøhus complex (1939) is

Completed in 1941 (Figs 4.3 and 4.4), this was the largest such municipal facility built in Denmark since the Copenhagen City Hall. As an emblem of effective modern urban democracy the role of the city hall serves three main purposes: first, to provide chambers for the city council; second, to appropriately house the administrative offices of the city; and third, to function as a stage for the ceremonial activities of the city.

With those three programmatic requirements the city hall is organized with three major blocks placed asymmetrically in typical Functionalist fashion (Fig. 4.3). The site is in an urban park next to a major street. The first block, projecting into the park, contains the council chamber, ceremonial 'Marriage Hall' and main entrance lobby. The middle and largest block houses the administrative offices and runs parallel to the street. The final block, set against a side street, serves the public directly as the place to pay for city services, make inquiries or obtain information. The clock tower becomes the fourth element. While the entire building is sheathed in a patterned grey Norwegian marble and has similar-sized repetitive window elements, each block has distinguishing features.

The cubic ceremonial block incorporates an extended entry element housing the council chamber on the second level. The four-storey entrance hall connects the administrative wing with the ceremonial hall, while shielding the council chamber behind the two-storey mural *Human Society* (1947) by Thorvald Hagedorn-Olsen. The four-storey ceremonial 'Marriage Hall' (Fig. 4.4) has a finely detailed interior with curved skylights and a full-height window facing the park. Wood panelling finishes all the

Fig. 4.3 Arne Jacobsen and Erik Møller's City Hall (1941) in Aarhus illustrates modifications to Functionalist organizational principles through the use of regional materials and building traditions. While each function of the programme is articulated as a distinct element, the use of grey Norwegian granite and repetitive windows binds the composition together. (Photo: By martinwm (Own work) [CC BY-SA 3.0 (http://creativecommons.org/licenses/by-sa/3.0)], via Wikimedia Commons)

Fig. 4.4 The ceremonial 'Marriage Hall' demonstrates Jacobsen's control of both interior space and refined detailing in Aarhus City Hall. The curved skylights bathe the room in the changing natural light from outside while the wood panelling and flooring supply a sense of warmth to the space. (Photo: By Seier+Seier (arne jacobsen, aarhus town hall 1937–1942) [CC BY 2.0 (http://creativecommons.org/licenses/by/2.0)], via Wikimedia Commons)

public spaces, complemented by a herringbone-patterned wood floor. The detailing is exquisite, especially in the ceremonial hall, with its off-white structure and skylights complementing the panelling.

The administrative wing is a long, narrow block articulated by the repetitive rhythm of square windows and capped by a sloped copper roof. As the largest of the functional elements and executed in a singular material with repetitive fenestration, it truly reads as the administrative or bureaucratic unit. A unique interior spatial response avoids having boring double-loaded corridors by incorporating a thin multi-storey sky-lit atrium that brings light

into a four-storey office circulation space. The material palette of warm wooden panels, brass fixtures and exposed white structural system provides a suitable interactive space for the office workers.

The smallest element is where the public goes to pay bills and obtain information and this has large window openings and a curved roof form providing a sense of openness and accessibility. The last element in the composition, the clock tower, was not part of the original competition entry for the city hall and was added in 1941. The public demand for a tower was so intense it forced the architects to acquiesce and add the tower,

resulting in a 60-metre-high modernist structural frame with an enormous clock face placed mid-way up the tower.

The Aarhus City Hall truly celebrates the synthesis of Functionalist planning and design concepts with regional materials and forms. While the exterior has been criticized for its seeming austerity – the cool grey Norwegian granite and repetitious window patterning – the interiors use organic materials and curved forms coupled with highly refined detailing. The furnishings and fixtures were all designed by Jacobsen and achieve an extraordinary level of quality and craftsmanship.

a more multifaceted composition. The handmade red brick planar façade provides a datum that is carved into while simultaneously having cantilevered white horizontal balconies. Horizontal windows run along the façade and then turn into the balconies, creating a sense of transparency.

Two town halls by Arne Jacobsen further demonstrate how regional norms modify Functionalist tenets. The first is the large, urbane and iconic Aarhus City Hall (1941) by Jacobsen and Erik Møller (see 'The Aarhus City Hall') (Figs 4.3 and 4.4). The second and more modest Søllerød Town Hall (1942), by Jacobsen and Flemming Lassen, is located on a suburban site next to a wood. The building form expresses the programme explicitly; the larger executive or bureaucratic wing intersects with the smaller block housing the entry, council chamber and public reception spaces. Both blocks are clad in grey Norwegian marble with sloped copper roofs. Repetitive punched window openings regulate the administrative wing, while the extended entry and the two-storey council chamber have larger vertical fenestration. Bronze bells accompany an etched clock face on the façade of the council chamber. The interior furnishings, light fixtures and textiles were designed by Jacobsen. Here, like in the Aarhus University and Nyborg Library, the limited material palette and window articulation creates a subtle, refined dignity.

In Finland, Gunnar Taucher's straightforward red brick and ribbon-windowed customs warehouse (1938) on the Katakanokka wharf in Helsinki harbour and the elementally composed red brick Kesko headquarters (1940) in Helsinki by Toivo Paatela combine Functionalist composition with tactile local materials, achieving sophisticated results. Erik Bryggman's Sampo Insurance headquarters (1936) and Resurrection Chapel (1940), both in Turku, also exemplify this vernacularized modernism. The Insurance headquarters, while referencing Functionalism with its glazed two-storey ground-floor level that appears to support the heavier mass above, is constructed of masonry with punched window openings for the upper floors. But it is the chapel where Bryggman's full expressive

Fig. 4.5 The interior of the Bryggman's Resurrection Chapel, seen through the leafy metal screen, brings light from the colonnaded side space and altar area while allowing views into the cemetery and nature. (Photo: Author)

creativity is achieved. The simple sloped roofed building form, finished in white painted stucco, has a marble-tiled loggia, flagstone paving and sculptured stone entrance (see Fig. 4.1). The foyer, with a metal vine sculptured grille on the inner glass door, provides filtered views into the chapel (Fig. 4.5). The chapel, with a curved ceiling, has seating on one side while the light from outside accents the altar area and draws one's view out to the cemetery and nature. Dark/light, smooth/rough, modern/archaic; in addition to embracing a number of architectural qualities, these dualities capture the rich range of human emotions, associations and feelings aptly synthesized in space and form by Bryggman.

In Norway, Finn Bryn and Johan Ellefsen's buildings for the lower part of the Blindern Campus (1935) of the University of Oslo blend modernism's cubic volumetrics with excellently detailed brickwork and expressive fenestration that responds to the varied functions within each building. In Sweden, Olof Thunström's Höjdhagen housing complex (1940) in Gustavsberg outside of Stockholm and Harry Egler's yellow brick and stained-wood row houses (1939) in the Stocksund suburb of Stockholm, incorporate regional materials and forms. The chapels of

St Knut and St Gertrud (1944) in Malmö's Eastern Cemetery, by Sigurd Lewerentz, use thin bands of marble on the exterior, while weaving marble with yellow brick and pine ribs in the interior, creating an intense tactility.

In these works we see the return of tactility and materiality and a movement away from the abstract machine imagery of the 1920s and 1930s. Palpability and corporeal presence returned to Scandinavian architecture, along with a freer, more varied handling of forms and spaces. This undercurrent of regional influence demonstrated that a modern architecture with roots in a specific place was possible.

Asplund and the Aaltos versus Functionalism

For Alvar and Aino Aalto and Erik Gunnar Asplund, regional forms and traditions did not get to the root of the issue; their critique of modernism was more instrumental. The Aaltos and Asplund were concerned about the impact of mechanization on the human spirit, represented by Functionalism's reliance upon universal technique, serial production and machine imagery. Modernism resulted in architecture that contributed to the ever-increasing alienation experienced by the individual in modern mass society. They questioned the idea that industrialized society could create a better life for people than nature could.

Criticizing Functionalist architecture, Aalto stated in his 1935 lecture 'Rationalism and Man': 'We have conceded and we should be agreed upon the fact that objects properly can be given the label *rational* often suffer from a notable lack of human qualities [*sic*].'[29] By 1940, in his essay 'The Humanization of Architecture', he emphatically stated: 'Technical functionalism cannot create definite architecture'.[30] Asplund's 1936 speech, 'Art and Technology', contains similar sentiments: 'One should not conceive of utility as an end in itself but merely as a means to increase choice and well-being for people in this life. Technology does not suffice to achieve this ...'.[31]

Neither the Aaltos nor Asplund suggested the rejection of industrial production per se; rather they questioned its use as a design strategy. They proposed a more humane architecture, one transcending the abstract qualities of Functionalism. Nor were they promoting a nostalgic traditionalism or historicism. They sought an architecture that would mediate between the universality of modern civilization and the specifics of local culture.

The modern individual's separation from nature was a primary concern of both. To address this, they desired to reconnect the individual with the biological structures and rhythms of the natural world. To foster more direct participation with nature, they reasserted the importance of place, physically and culturally, in their work. More than enhancing a site, they actively cultivated it, paying specific attention to the particulars of the local condition. Asplund and the Aaltos appealed to the full range of human experiences, memories and perceptions by employing a variety of sensory and tactile qualities in their designs, favouring a more corporeal and tangible materiality rooted in the norms of local tradition and usage.

Several of Erik Gunnar Asplund's works designed before his untimely death in 1940 demonstrated his new direction. While this included the crematoria at Kviberg (1940) and Skövde (1940), two works capture it best: the Gothenburg Law Courts addition (1937) and the Woodland Crematorium (1940).[32] Through their very different programmes and contexts, they demonstrate Asplund's ability to reimagine the vital heritages of the past as well as revitalizing the experiential and tactile capacities of architecture.

Asplund's Law Courts addition to Nicodemus Tessin's 1672 Gothenburg City Hall accepts the urban, neoclassical context of Gustaf Adolf Square as binding. The exterior of the addition provides a contemporary interpretation of Tessin's classical façade; a patterned structural frame whose proportions and rhythms are based on the original building (Fig. 4.6). Asplund's structural grid, though modern

Fig. 4.6 Erik Gunnar Asplund's Law Courts addition (1937) in Gothenburg interprets the original neoclassical façade in a modern yet respectful manner, creating a regulated wholeness to the composition. (Photo: Author)

in appearance and construction, is further regulated both vertically and horizontally by the order of the original neoclassical façade. The result is a compositional wholeness, yet each frame reads as a temporally different structure. The neutrality of the new structural grid emphasizes its subordinate relationship to the original city hall and the other historic buildings in the square.

The interior of the addition extends the existing exterior courtyard into the composition, forming a light-filled atrium surrounded by courtroom spaces (Fig. 4.7). The atrium incorporates figural or curved forms, spaces and elements, with walls and balustrades finished in wood panelling. The interior concrete structure, stairs, elevator and clock are cream-coloured and, when combined with the wood-panelled surfaces, convey a tactility and tangibility that speaks to the civic and social propriety of the space. The skylight bathes the atrium in the

Fig. 4.7 The refined sky-lit atrium of the Law Courts addition is finished in warm wood panelling with white-painted structural elements. The skylight bathes the atrium in the ever-changing light from the Swedish sky. (Photo: By B****n (Own work) [CC BY 3.0 (http://creativecommons.org/licenses/by/3.0)], via Wikimedia Commons)

Fig. 4.8 A comprehensive vista is presented in the approach to Erik Gunnar Asplund's Woodland Crematorium (1940) in Stockholm. The buildings seem subordinated to the dramatic, seemingly naturalist, landscape. (Photo: By Holger.Ellgaard (Own work) [CC BY-SA 3.0 (http://creativecommons.org/licenses/by-sa/3.0)], via Wikimedia Commons)

ever-changing light from the Swedish sky, a constant reminder of the daily and yearly cycles of the natural world outside. Here Asplund responds to the local condition, both physically and culturally.

Within a gently sloping landscape contained by dark forest edges, Asplund presents a comprehensive vista to those approaching the Woodland Crematorium. An ensemble composed of strategically placed elements is offered: a processional walk, low wall, loggia, dark cross and a meditation grove placed on a raised mound (Fig. 4.8). The naturalistic aspects of the site appear dominant, for the buildings seem subordinated to the dramatic landscape. But Asplund did more than enhance the site features; he recrafted a former gravel pit into a resonant dialogue between landscape and architecture. The vitality of this dialogue is fostered by the open vistas that frame the architectural elements as they stand discretely in the space of the site.

A long, low wall leads to the classically inspired loggia crowning the complex. Courtyards and a layered series of walls form the two smaller chapels; both wall and courtyard are common elements associated with Swedish vernacular building complexes. The loggia is balanced across the landscape by a tree-bedecked meditation mound, while the wayfarer's cross acts as a vertical counterpoint between the two. The cave-like interior of the main chapel contrasts the openness of the loggia, while the loggia

gestures to the earthen hill of the meditation mound, recalling ancient Scandinavian burial mounds (Fig. 4.9). The materials used in the complex reinforce the contrasting character of the elements: the varied verdure of the landscape, the rough stone walk, smooth stucco wall surfaces, cream-coloured stone walls and columns, dark granite cross, wood beams and grey stucco and concrete. In addition to bringing forth a number of cultural associations, Asplund's use of material conveys a full range of experiential and tactile qualities and associations, reinforcing the corporeal nature of the entire experience.

Both of these seminal works demonstrated Asplund's intent to reincorporate the cultural heritages of the past through establishing place, as well as revitalizing the experiential and tactile capacities of architecture. This is a resonant architecture that eschewed the trivializing character of a nostalgic, or allusion-based, architecture.

The Aaltos' work begins to assume a more personal and expressive direction with the Viipuri Library (now in Vyborg, Russia), their own house and studio (1936) in Helsinki, the Finnish Pavilions for the 1937 Paris World's Fair and 1939 New York World's Fair and the Villa Mairea (1939) in Noormarkku. At this time and in these works, the themes that characterized the Aaltos' mature work over the next three decades emerged: the use of undulating and sinuous elements and forms; a rich vocabulary

Fig. 4.9 Nearing sunset, looking from the Woodland Crematorium loggia across the landscape to the sacred grove on the mnemonic meditation mound, one senses the onset of a mood or atmosphere beginning to imbue the place. (Photo: Krysta Mae Dimick)

Small Rehearsals of Form: Alvar and Aino Aalto's Applied Designs

From spatial construct to building form, sinuosity is a unique characteristic of the Aaltos' architecture. Moreover, one sees similar qualities in the designs they produced for their furniture, glass vases and light fixtures. When they moved their office from Turku to Helsinki in 1933, they enjoyed an international reputation based upon their *Turun Sanomat* newspaper building and the Paimio Tuberculosis Sanatorium (*see* Fig. 3.10) as well as their furniture and applied designs (*see* 'The Paimio Sanatorium'). In the late 1920s the Aaltos collaborated with Otto Korhonen, the technical manager of a Turku joinery firm, on furniture production. Their initial partnership produced a stackable chair

and from this followed a series of chairs characterized by moulded curved forms made of laminated wood. In 1929 they produced a one-piece moulded plywood seat and back intended for serial production.

The next design problem was creating a wooden frame to support the continuous seat and back that could maintain its shape and be mass-produced. In the early 1930s a series of sculpture-like experiments investigating the shaping potentials of laminated wood were undertaken. These abstract sculptures captured in three-dimensional form the sensuous and expressive qualities emerging in their architecture at the time.

In the iconic 'Paimio' chair (1932), the single-piece moulded seat and back is supported by laminated birch sides that have been formed into a continuous curve (Fig. 4.10). This was furniture moulded in wood from the Finnish forest that could be serially produced. Continuing to engage in sculptural wood experiments, they developed a number of furniture designs for the Viipuri Library (1935). The Aaltos produced specific furniture designs for their numerous architecture projects, many put into mass production. In 1935 the Aaltos, with Maire Gullichsen and Nils-Gustaf Hahl, formed ARTEK, whose aim was to promote their furniture and glassware and to produce the furniture.

of skylight and clerestory forms developed to bring in natural light into interior spaces; spatial differentiation between the important public and civic spaces and the support spaces within the building programme; and the use of courtyards or atriums as a primary organizational device for buildings and complexes.[34]

While no longer extant, the two World's Fair pavilions immersed the Aaltos in examining what defined Finnish culture and how to express it, as the pavilions needed to capture and present a sense of 'Finnish-ness'. For the Paris Fair the complex was ordered about a courtyard, with the major exhibition space sheathed in wooden batten cladding and surmounted by circular skylights. The New York pavilion was dominated by a three-storey undulating, stepped wooden wall that contained photographic

essays of the Finnish landscape, people and products (importantly, wood products). Submitted under the competition name 'Aurora Borealis', the evocative sinuous form captured, metaphorically, the qualities of the lake landscape of Finland, the dancing Northern Lights and the importance of wood in Finnish society and culture.

In the Viipuri Library two large blocks defined the simple massing of the whitewashed brick building, yet revealed few clues to the spatial dynamics found within. The larger volume houses the library hall with reading room. A dramatic staircase with a tactile wooden handrail binds the tiered floor levels together. This open, light-coloured multi-level space is surmounted by fifty-eight circular skylights, each 6 feet (1.80m) deep, that provide a shadow-free diffused light for reading. This form of skylight becomes a

Alvar continued to design furniture after Aino's untimely death in 1949.

The Aalto name became associated with glassware in 1932, when Aino won second place in a competition sponsored by two Finnish glass manufacturers for a glass tableware series. The series won her a gold medal at the 1936 Milan Triennale. In 1933, Alvar won second place in a competition with a nesting set of glass tableware called the 'Riihimäki Flower'. For the 1937 Paris World's Fair, the Aaltos produced an irregularly shaped curved-form vase that became the precursor of the famous 'Savoy Vase'. These sinuous configured glass forms, as well as the continuously curved furniture elements, resemble the undulating shapes that were appearing contemporaneously in

their architecture: the entry canopies in the Paimio Sanatorium and Villa Maria, the undulating ceiling in the Viipuri Library and the giant curved exhibition wall in the 1939 Finnish Pavilion for the New York World's Fair. The undulating, sinuous space, form and building elements came to characterize the Aaltos' architecture, with the seeds for this unique expressive vocabulary being rooted in the furniture and glassware designs of the 1930s.[33]

Fig. 4.10 Alvar Aalto's Armchair 41 'Paimio' (1932) is composed of a sinuous single-piece curved seat and back combined with the curved laminated supports that are serially produced wood products from the Finnish forest. (Photo: Courtesy Artek (Armchair 41 'Paimio Chair', Design Alvar Aalto, 1932, © Artek)

Fig. 4.11 The interior courtyard of Alvar and Aino Aalto's Villa Mairea (1939) in Noormarku, organized around the sauna plunge pool, recalls an opening in a Finnish meadow, being by a Finnish lake, or even a vernacular farm courtyard. Here numerous dual tectonic images, such as modern/traditional, rough/smooth and permanent/ephemeral are experienced. (Photo: Author)

signature feature in numerous future Aalto buildings. The smaller volume houses the entry foyer, library offices and the public meeting room with its full-length glazed wall to its green park setting and unforgettable and powerful sinuous, flowing red Karelian pine ceiling.

The Aaltos' home and studio and the Villa Mairea (Figs 4.11 and 4.12) are works further demonstrating the architects' movement away from Functionalism. Their house and studio combines whitewashed brick with wood siding (cladding) and is organized with a garden courtyard in the rear. But it is the Villa Mairea[35] that synthesizes and transforms the heritages and traditions of place into a multivalent work of architecture. The villa carves a place in the Finnish forest by forming an L-shaped building block around an exterior courtyard containing an undulating shaped plunge pool for the sauna (Fig. 4.11). The courtyard is a mnemonic device, as it recalls both a forest meadow and lake, in addition to the courtyards around which traditional Finnish farm complexes are organized. The materials used

in the complex include whitewashed brick for the support areas of the villa and wood, tile and stone for the public spaces. The detailing is machine-like for some elements, yet vernacular for others. The flowing interior spaces are again a rich tapestry of textures, materials and associations, including the use of vertical poles in the interior spaces to provide a sense of being in the forest. Throughout the villa, dualities of smooth/textured, modern/traditional, light/dark and inside/outside engage the individual in a stimulating offering of experiential qualities and conditions (Fig. 4.12).

These works demonstrate the Aaltos' humanistic intent to reintegrate the individual with nature while revitalizing the experiential qualities of architecture. What began as the mastering of an international style for the Aaltos became transformed into an architecture that provided a true closeness with nature. While Asplund and the Aaltos sought to recapture architecture's role in everyday life by returning to the tangible realities of place, experience and memory, many Scandinavian architects

Fig. 4.12 The exterior of the Villa Mairea exhibits a rich material palette using wood, stone and large glazed areas to articulate the living or honorific spaces of the villa while using white stucco for its secondary spaces. Here, too, the dual tectonic imagery continues. (Photo: Author)

continued to use traditional norms and local materials to modify Functionalist ideas. These architects did not relinquish using industrial technique as a design strategy; rather they continued to balance modernist tenets with regional building traditions and local conditions. Following World War II, this represented one of the several major directions that Nordic architecture would take.

Chapter 5

POST-WAR EXPLORATION: A MATURING AND EXPANDING MODERNISM (1945–70)

IN THE IMMEDIATE AFTERMATH OF THE SECOND World War, Scandinavian countries emerged as social models representing progressive modern societies. The war had led to destruction and suffering in Finland, Norway and Denmark, while Sweden had come through relatively unscathed. The welfare state model was coalescing, characterized by a strong central government and an ideology of equality. The ideal was everyone had equal rights, regardless of background and social or economic status, and would be provided equal access to communally created societal goods and services.

Functionalism had been directly associated with the emergence of the welfare state before the war and continued as an important instrument participating in this social transformation. The principles of the Nordic model were secured by a large state or state-supported sector that subsidized industrialization and modernization by building housing for a variety of social and economic situations, as well as institutions and facilities for education, cultural life, childcare and eldercare and sports and recreation. The architectural ideas of Functionalism assisted in realizing a societal vision that created a unique modern architecture. Because of these democratic social conditions modern architecture continued to thrive, developing into a mature form.

Following the war, Scandinavian architecture and applied design achieved important international recognition. Architects sought to create an architecture respecting both place and tradition while maintaining a modernist trajectory. The use of particular local materials, especially brick, wood and copper, coupled with the continued responsiveness to the character

and features of place, cemented a homogeneous view of Northern developments. It was an architecture characterized by social engagement and a high quality of execution in its design and construction. Viewed from without, Nordic countries appeared to have a design unity and common direction; modern architecture in the North had become mature and responsive. It seemed to synthesize individuality, variation and standardization, in addition to fostering a variety of forms of expression.

For Nordic architects post-war architecture was not homogeneous, for rather than moving monolithically in a single route several different directions began to develop. The modified vernacularized modernism from the late 1930s was continued and expanded by a number of more mature practitioners: many of these works were executed in yellow or red brick depending on the country. For younger practitioners, synthesizing local brick traditions with the organizational, material and aesthetic concepts of British brutalism and the post-war concrete architecture of Le Corbusier provided a more expressive and poetic direction. In continuing modernism's focus on rationalism and industrial production, other architects explored the technical expression and curtain-wall construction systems seen in post-war American corporate high-rise buildings. This was best exemplified by the work of Mies van der Rohe, who had migrated to the United States from Germany in 1937. There was also an interest in creating a dynamic architecture which was in close contact with nature, was responsive to site and used traditional materials. Here the American architect Frank Lloyd Wight and the traditional architecture

Fig. 5.1 The Swedish new town of Vällingby (1948–60) by Backström and Reinius illustrates how a satellite community linked to Stockholm by subway can simultaneously provide access to nature. The new towns had commercial and civic buildings in addition to a variety of housing types. (Photo: Cogg bildbyrå (Sven Markelius, arkitekt. Arkitektur Förlag) [Public domain], via Wikimedia Commons)

of Japan provided inspiration. While it is interesting to note the many external ideas influencing Nordic architects, simultaneously, there were expressive individual personalities such as Arne Jacobsen, Jørn Utzon, Sigurd Lewerentz, Sverre Fehn, Alvar Aalto and Reima and Raili Pietilä, among others.

While post-war reconstruction occurred throughout Europe, housing and new town planning held a particular place in the Nordic countries following the war. Building and planning types were primarily determined by political and social conditions and generated by a variety of state, provincial and local agencies. Housing is an important political domain for the welfare state and so too the control of the conditions in which housing projects are initiated and developed. Unique to the North is the notion that more than any other type of construction housing is determined by the prevailing political and social conditions. The architectural contribution then emerges from the legal, financial, planning and technical considerations established by the commissioning governmental entity. Within this context, housing and new town planning projects executed throughout Scandinavia provided fresh models for well-organized urban, suburban and rural growth (*see* Figs 5.1, 5.2, 5.3 and 6.16).

Denmark

Danish architects explored the variety of directions Nordic architecture took following the war, from

Fig. 5.2 The extensive red brick housing complex at Dronningegården (1958) in Copenhagen, by Kay Fisker (with C.F. Møller and Svenn Eske Kristensen), exemplifies the tradition of a vernacularized modernism common in Denmark following the Second World War. (Photo: By Seier+Seier [CC BY 2.0 (http://creativecommons.org/licenses/by/2.0)], via Wikimedia Commons)

expanding their vernacularized modernism to incorporating European, America and Japanese influences. What provided common focus for the Danes was architecture communicating craftsmanship, simplicity and objectivity, regardless of its aesthetic or formal expression. As Kay Fisker commented about post-war Nordic architecture: 'It is not pretentious and bombastic as in the Latin countries, monumentality is not an end in itself, we strive for an architecture that serves life and humanity, which subordinates itself to nature, does not obtrude, but on the contrary wants to be anonymous.'[36]

The vernacularized modernism of the Aarhus University complex by Fisker, Stegmann and Møller continued in the post-war era. All Fisker's works were preoccupied with usefulness, order, good craftsmanship and objectivity. His extensive red brick housing complex at Dronningegården (1943–58, with C.F. Møller and Svenn Eske Kristensen) (Fig. 5.2) and the indigenous yellow brick Voldparken housing estate (1951), both in Copenhagen, continue the restrained expressiveness of Aarhus. Two other important works in Copenhagen executed in yellow brick, are the programmatically expressive Voldparken School (1953)

and the Young Mothers' Assistance building (1961) with its studied form and refined detailing.

A number of architects executed works in this vernacularized modernism. Palle Suenson's Smidth Company headquarters (1956), while simple and rational in plan, has powerful façades comprising narrow vertical brick columns and full-height recessed windows. Copenhagen city architect F.C. Lund, with his colleague Hans Christian Hansen, executed two works that combine modern programmatic and spatial ordering with traditional materials and forms: the Hanssted School (1958) in Copenhagen and the Ringbo Nursing Home (1964) in Bagsværd. Inger and Johannes Exner's yellow brick St Clemens Church (1963) in Randers has a sanctuary expressing the idea of hands in prayer. Ejnar Borg's yellow brick Skagen Town Hall (1968) is a symphony of pitched red tile roof forms, while Viggo Møller-Jensen and Tyge Arnfred's Klarskovgård (1970), the educational centre at Korsør, combines traditional brick forms with sloped tile roofs.

While one of Jørn Utzon's first works was the tripod-shaped Svaneke water tower (1951) in Bornholm, it was the courtyard housing complexes at

Fig. 5.3 Jørn Utzon's Fredensborg housing complex (1962) is like a small village nestled into its site and built with traditional Danish forms and regional materials. (Photo: By Ramblersen (Own work) [CC BY-SA 3.0 (http://creativecommons.org/licenses/by-sa/3.0)], via Wikimedia Commons)

Kingo (1958) and Fredensborg (1962) that established his reputation (Fig. 5.3). Sensitively sited, both combine traditional Danish forms and regional materials with Japanese and Wrightian spatial qualities. The two complexes, constructed of yellow brick with yellow roofing tiles, appear as small, well-scaled villages in the landscape, both using L-shaped living units formed around a brick-paved exterior courtyard. Utzon's larger works included the high-rise Elineberg housing towers (1966) in Helsingborg and the expressive Hammershøj Care Centre (1966) in Helsingør. But it is the Sydney Opera House (1957–74), with its expressive shell structure, that Utzon was best known for at the time. The project's complications and Utzon's eventual resignation from the commission are well documented.[37] (See 'The Minimalist House: Glass, Steel or Wood and Little Else' on additional Utzon works.)

Arne Jacobsen executed two housing projects and a school combining yellow brick with traditional forms: the Søholm row houses (1950) in Bellevue, the Allé housing (1952) in Copenhagen and the Munkegaard School (1956) with its chequerboard pattern of classrooms and courtyards. But the majority of his post-war works were rational, technically exquisite buildings demonstrating Miesian influences which included prismatic forms, sophisticated curtain-wall systems and excellent detailing. Achieving harmony between foreign influences and domestic tradition, Jacobsen's work captured the Danish desire for simple order, thoroughness of detailing and care in execution. The refined grey glass and stainless-steel curtain wall of the Rødovre Town Hall

(1955) is complemented by the excellently detailed interior glass staircases. The Jespersen & Sons office building (1955) in Copenhagen clearly demonstrates Jacobsen's mastery of contemporaneous American corporate architecture. But it was the Copenhagen SAS Royal Hotel (1961) that exemplified his capacity to create a showpiece of total design, for it is universally recognized for its exquisite furniture and tableware designs as for its architecture (Fig. 5.4) (*see* 'Arne Jacobsen's Total Design Aesthetic'). Jacobsen's Danish National Bank (1971) combines rational spatial planning with an expressive and refined use of stone and glass.

Other Danish architects who executed works influenced by Mies and American corporate architecture include: Bornebusch, Brüel and Selchau's large and extensive Copenhagen County Hospital (1960–76) at Herlev; Henning Larsen's Trondheim University Campus Centre (1968) with its interior pedestrian streets; Viggo Møller-Jensen's curtain-walled apartment house (1952) in Frederiksberg; Halldor Gunnløgsson and Jørn Nielsen's Tårnby Town Hall (1960) in Copenhagen, with an expressed glazed council chamber; Erik Christian Sørensen and Mogens Boertmann's Virum Pharmacy (1953) in Lyngby with its colourful curtain wall; and Nils and Eva Koppel's elegantly executed glass and steel Langelinie Pavilion (1958) in Copenhagen and their concrete and glass Technical University of Denmark (1959–74) in Lundtofte.

Not content to merely follow Kay Fisker's vernacular modification of modernism, a number of architects were influenced by British brutalist aesthetics

Fig. 5.4 Arne Jacobsen's post-war works were rational, technically exquisite buildings demonstrating influences from Mies van der Rohe and American commercial architecture. His SAS Royal Hotel (1961), with its aluminium curtain wall with green and grey glass, exemplified his capacity to create a showpiece of total design. (Photo: Author)

house with vaulted roof at Julsø (1968) which was inspired by Le Corbusier's Maison Jaoul; Henning Larsen's concrete Chapel of Rest (1967) in Aarhus; and Ib and Jørgen Rasmussen's red brick Buddinge Church (1969, with Ole Meyer) in Copenhagen, with its layered parallel planar walls.

Jean-Jacques Baruël worked in the Aalto office in Helsinki in the 1950s and entered a number of competitions with Alvar. In his own practice he produced the City Hall (1969) in Nyköping, Sweden and the red brick Sønderborg Business School (1968), both exhibiting influences from his Aalto experiences. The red brick Teachers' Training College (1965) in Aalborg, by Nils Andersen and Salli Besiakow, also exhibits Aaltoesque qualities.

Karen and Ebbe Clemmensen's Blågård College (1966) and Enghavegård School (1966), both with Jørgen Bo, have a more Functionalist appearance, with glazed façades and flat roofs, while their swimming facilities at Kildeskovhallen (1972) in Gentofte present an elegant blend of large expanses of glazing with traditional masonry elements. The LO-School (1969) in Helsingør is organized about a central atrium with pitched-roof forms of various sizes to articulate the differing programmatic needs.

Representing a more organic direction is Bo and Wohlert's Louisiana Museum of Art (1958, with expansions in 1966, 1971 and 1982) which powerfully fuses nature, architecture and art. (The museum name came from Alexander Brun, who called the orginal villa and property 'Louisiana' after his three wives, all named Louise.) Here the building seems subservient to the landscape, a modest intervention, while blending both Japanese and Miesian influences. Another work that synthesizes multiple influences is Karen and Ebbe Clemmensen's Skive Teachers' Training College (1960), with its Miesian structural regularity, Wrightian roofs and overhangs and Japanese material and experiential qualities.

During the post-war period, the Danish government built numerous high-density residential complexes, including Søndergaardsparken (1950) by Povl Ernst Hoff and Bennet Windinge, with a variety of

and use of expressive concrete and red brick. Friis & Moltke executed a number of exemplary red brick works including the secondary school in Vylby-Risskov (1969), the Hotel Lakolk (1966) in Rømø and the education centre Scanticon (1973) near Aarhus. These works featured expressive concrete structures and dynamic public spaces, coupled with numerous skylights to animate the interiors. Other examples include Nils and Eva Koppel's Søllerød Park housing (1956) in North Zealand; Mogens Lassen's red brick

Many modern architects engaged in designing furniture, housewares, light fixtures and fabrics among other items for daily use. The intent was often to ensure a comprehensive aesthetic that integrated everyday objects with their architecture, as well as for general commercial production. As part of Arne Jacobsen's concept of total design and seen in his SAS Royal Hotel (now the Radisson Blu Royal Hotel) (Fig. 5.4), he set a unique standard for a high quality of production. From the aluminium curtain wall with its green and grey glass, through to the stainless-steel cutlery used in the restaurant, to the 'Swan' and 'Egg' chairs gracing the lobby, all was under Jacobsen's control (Fig. 5.5).

Shades of green dominated the entire design; green textiles and furniture are combined with 'organic shapes' in creative tension with rigid geometric architectural forms. The furniture pieces created specifically for the hotel included the iconic 'Egg' and 'Swan' chairs (Fig. 5.5) designed in 1958 and the 'Swan' sofa. Jacobsen later designed a table series to complement these pieces. While his furniture originally populated the hotel and all its guest rooms, today only a single room (#606) has been kept with its original colour scheme, furniture and wood panelling.

Other Jacobsen furniture designs that continue to be serially

produced include the well-known 'Ant' chair and accompanying 'Dot' stools, the 'Grand Prix' chair and the 'Series 7' chair. He also designed the 'Silver Matte' cutlery collection, the 'Cylinda-line' tableware series in stainless steel and a number of light fixtures. It is the care and attention to both the idea and its execution that characterizes the high quality of these designs by Jacobsen, be it a building or a set of cutlery. All his designs are well thought out, thoroughly studied, thoughtfully executed and exquisitely realized. That his furniture and objects for everyday use are considered design classics and many are still in production attests to their timelessness.

Fig. 5.5 Jacobsen's concept of total design included designing furniture, housewares, light fixtures and fabrics as part of the overall building conception. The three chairs – the 'Drop', the 'Egg' and the 'Swan' – were all designed in 1958 for the SAS Royal Hotel, pictured in the background, as too was the fabric displayed here. (Photo: By lglazier618 (Fritz Hansen) [CC BY 2.0 (http://creativecommons.org/licenses/by/2.0)], via Wikimedia Commons)

housing types; Bredalsparken (1954) in Hvidovre using traditional materials and forms by Eske Kristensen; and the mixed-use complex Høje Gladsaxe (1968) by Hoff and Windinge with a consortium of others. As a critique of these large complexes, architects begin proposing low-rise, traffic-separated and courtyard housing complexes, exemplified by Fællestegnestuen (1966) in Albertslund South designed by Viggo Møller-Jensen.

Sweden

Sweden, the emblematic welfare state, developed seminal new town planning projects, with Vällingby (1948–64) (*see* Fig. 5.1) and Farsta (1956–60) designed by Backström and Reinius being the most recognized examples. Based upon late nineteenth-century British garden-city concepts where satellite towns were linked to the city by railways, these Swedish new towns provided both access to nature and subway connection to Stockholm. Further, they combined housing, commercial and civic buildings within an architecture capturing both modernity and tradition, albeit somewhat nostalgic at times. While Backström and Reinius did the planning for the new towns and some of the buildings, a number of Swedish architects executed projects within each.

The development of various-sized housing estates was critical to the welfare state and most provided a variety of housing types. The intent was to create visually stimulating complexes as well as maximizing individual family choice. In the Kortedala suburb of Gothenburg is a complex of five twelve-storey triangular towers (1957) by Brolid and Wallinder; the triangular shape maximized solar exposure. In Örebro, Baronbackarna (1957) by Ekholm and White integrates shopping, schools and social services with low-rise housing executed in a vernacularized modernism using traditional materials. Backström and Reinius had extensive experience in housing estates before embarking on their two new town projects; in Stockholm they executed Danviksklippan (1945), with

its nine tower blocks, and Gröndal (1944–62) with its interesting mix of terrace housing, row housing and tower blocks. Beginning in the early 1960s the Swedes began the *Miljonprogrammet* or Million Programme to build a million housing units to ensure that everyone could have a home at a reasonable price.

While Nils Tesch and L.M. Giertz's Solna High School (1947) combined a vernacularized modern exterior with a large white Functionalist interior atrium, it was Peter Celsing, among others, who fused vernacular modernism with the red brick and exposed concrete aesthetic of British brutalism. Celsing created a number of striking, expressive red brick churches; including the Härlanda Church (1959) in Gothenburg, the St Thomas Church (1959) in Vällingby, the Oscar Parish Church (1959) in Stockholm and the Almtuna Church (1959) in Uppsala, along with the all-concrete boat-shaped St Olaf Nacksta Church (1969) in Sundsvall. He also executed two significant large-scale urban works in Stockholm, both in concrete and glass: the important cultural centre (1973) at Sergels Torg (Fig. 5.6) with its glass façade framing the sunken square, and the Swedish Film Institute (1970). Other brutalist-inspired works include Carl Nyrén's small concrete Västerort Church (1956) in Vällingby; Klas Anshelm's red brick Lund Art Gallery (1957) with its white sky-lit interior spaces, and his dark brick Lund City Hall (1966) which has Miesian-inspired glazed elements; and Borgström and Lindroos's red brick Söderled Church (1960) in Farsta and the concrete Kaknäs TV tower (1967) in Stockholm.

Two important brutalist-influenced works in Stockholm are the Swedish House (1969) and the People's Palace (1960), both in concrete, by Sven Markelius, while Erik and Tore Ahlsén's Community Hall (1965) and Krämaren department store with housing tower (1963), both in Örebro, provide additional examples. An important civic work, the red brick Kiruna City Hall (1962), by Artur von Schmalensee, has a wondrous steel clock tower and light-filled concrete and wood public atrium space referred to as 'Kiruna's living room'. Alf Engström,

Fig. 5.6 The large-scale concrete and glass Cultural Centre (1973) in Stockholm's Sergels Torg, by Peter Celsing, exemplifies the influence of British brutalism while being a significant civic work in the city's movement to revitalize its downtown. (Photo: By Holger.Ellgaard (Own work) [CC BY-SA 3.0 (http://creativecommons.org/licenses/by-sa/3.0)], via Wikimedia Commons

Gunnar Landberg, Bengt Larsson and Alvar Törneman's crematorium (1960) in Gävle has a rough-finished concrete wall encircling a refined steel and glass pavilion; brutalism meets Mies.

While seemingly brutalist, Sigurd Lewerentz's red brick churches of St Mark's (1960) in Björkhagen, a Stockholm suburb (Fig. 5.7), and St Peter's (1966) in Klippan explore the material properties of masonry in a highly sculptural and idiosyncratic manner. In these two buildings, Lewerentz worked in close collaboration with the craftsmen on the job site. While the exteriors of the churches were of brick with very thick joints, the vaulting undulating over the sanctuary spaces is formed between steel 'I' beams. His small flower kiosk (1969) in Malmö's Eastern Cemetery is a minimalist essay in concrete and glass.

Ralph Erskine, who moved from Britain to Sweden in 1939, was focused on creating architecture for extreme climates, particular the Nordic sub-arctic region. This is exemplified in his Borgafjäll tourist hotel (1948) in Lapland which expressively combined an organic organizational sensibility with traditional building materials. In Luleå, Sweden's first indoor

shopping centre (1954), he demonstrated concepts for creating responsive arctic buildings. While his Brittgården Tibro housing estate (1959–69) in Västergötland and Esperanza housing complex (1971) in Landskrona are more normative designs, Erskine's housing complex 'Ortdrivaren' (1961) in Kiruna, with its rhythmic forms, rounded corners, modelled roof forms and suspended balconies, became the model for his future housing projects in Sweden and elsewhere.

Sven Markelius's Trades Union Centre (1955), an early example of a curtain-wall building, contributed to the revitalization of an older section of central Stockholm. The curtain wall was unique in using operable windows. Inspired by American high-rise architecture Stockholm's extensive post-war urban development programme is exemplified by the Hötorgs office and commercial complex (1956) by David Helldén, Anders Tengbom, Sven Markelius, Erik Lallerstedt and Backström and Reinius (Fig. 5.8). The complex was formed by five eighteen-storey high-rise curtain-walled office slabs that marked the city's new commercial centre. Along with the Hötorgs

The Minimalist House: Glass, Steel or Wood and Little Else

As Le Corbusier's Villa Savoy was the paradigm for houses of the future during the 1920s and 1930s, Mies van der Rohe's Farnsworth House (1951) in Plano, Illinois, was the exemplar of the post-war modern house. A minimalist and rationalist essay in white steel and glass, the house influenced numerous architects on the Continent as well as in the United States, not to mention Nordic practitioners. In Scandinavia, a sensitivity to the site and landscape, coupled with the open flexibility of Japanese screen architecture, often combined with Miesian rational planning and austere aesthetics.

Common to the houses executed in the North are open floor plans and spatial systems, often with minimal room definition; a regularized column and beam structure with glass infill or sliding glazed panels; horizontal flat roofs; planar interior wall systems of a singular material when walls are present; and the strong sense of interior space flowing into the exterior landscape. These works appear as light footprints on the land and gather nature, with its changing light, atmosphere and seasonal transitions, into the living spaces.

In Denmark, where those ideas are synthesized with Danish moderation and clarity, Jørn Utzon's

residence (1952) in Hellebæk and the Middelboe House (1955) in Holte combine a systematic, rational wood structure with planar brick walls, large glazing panels and responsive site planning. Both Erik Christian Sørensen's house (1955) in Ordrup and Halldor Gunnløgsson's house (1958) in Rungsted express their debt to Miesian rational planning and Japanese lightness. In Norway, Arne Korsmo's three elegant glass and steel row houses in Oslo (1955, with Christian Norberg-Schulz) are light and sophisticated interpretations of Mies.

In Finland, due to the influence of Aulis Blomstedt, Miesian ideas

informed the work of a generation of post-war architects. Examples include Kirmo Mikkola's terraced studio houses (1968) in Järvenpää; Ilkka Salo's open-planned wooden summer cottage (1966) in Naantali; Lindqvist, Löfström & Uosukainen's wood and glass summer house (1965) on the Finnish south coast; and Mikkola and Juhani Pallasmaa's wood and glass Relander summer house (1966) in Muurame. Kristian Gullichsen and Pallasmaa created an austere modular house constructed of minimal prefabricated wooden elements entitled 'Moduli 225' (1970) (Fig. 5.9); variations of the house were presented in a number of exhibitions in Finland. It was last shown at the International Exhibition of Wood Architecture at the Pompidou Centre in Paris in 1979.

Fig. 5.9 Kristian Gullichsen and Juhani Pallasmaa's Moduli 225 Summer Exhibition Pavilion (1970) was a minimalist rational modular house constructed from prefabricated wooden components. While shown in a number of Finnish exhibitions this example was constructed near the Villa Mairea in the mid-1970s. (Photo: Courtesy of Juhani Pallasmaa, photo by Patrick Degommier)

Fig. 5.10 Knut Knutsen's Norwegian Embassy (1950) in Stockholm incorporates both Wrightian and Japanese influences in its organization and material expression. (Photo: By Holger.Ellgaard (Own work) [CC BY-SA 3.0 (http://creativecommons.org/licenses/by-sa/3.0)], via Wikimedia Commons)

complex a number of significant buildings in Stockholm expressed this rational, technical direction, including Erik and Tore Ahlsén's PUB department store (1959) with its glass façade; the more solid façade of the Åhléns department store (1964) by Backström and Reinius; and VBB Arkitektkontor's Werner-Gren research centre complex (1961) with its steel frame and curtain-wall tower and living quarters for guest researchers. Paul Hedqvist executed three important concrete and curtain-walled high-rise buildings: the Tax Authority office building (1960) and the Dagens Nyheter building (1964), Sweden's tallest building for many years, and the Kockums main building (1955) in Malmö. Nils Einar Eriksson's Folksam office tower (1959) in Stockholm incorporates Swedish marble with the metal and glass curtain wall, while Carl Nyrén's steel and glass city hall (1961) for Värnamo is Miesian in inspiration.

Norway

While Knut Knutsen and Arne Korsmo remained influential and productive practitioners in post-war Norway, the brutalist-inspired work of Lund and Slaatto, among others, coupled with the emergence of Sverre Fehn and his powerful personal form of expression, were important in determining the direction of Norwegian architecture.

Knut Knutsen's work took several directions. First, in his summer house (1948) and the Thorkelsens' summer house (1961), both in Portør, and the Bergendahls summer house (1960) in Tjøme, Knutsen successfully and expressively integrated nature and architecture. These works, along with his Norwegian embassy (1950) in Stockholm (Fig. 5.10), exhibit the influence of Wrightian and Japanese architecture. At the same time Knutsen produced more normative

Fig. 5.11 The St Hallvard Church (1966) in Oslo by Lund and Slaatto exhibits brick and concrete material expression influenced by British brutalism while its sloping concrete ceiling references Le Corbusier's post-war architecture. (Photo: Author)

office and business structures in Oslo: the Liberal House (1950), the Hotel Viking (1952, with Fredrik Winsnes) with its concrete frame and red brick infill panels and the curtain-walled People's House (1962). Bjørn Simonnæs's Brekkestranda Hotel (1970) in Sogn demonstrates similar organic organizational and material sensibilities as the early Knutsen summer houses.

Beyond the work described in 'The Minimalist House', Arne Korsmo's continued pursuit of active modernism was evident in his design of a series of temporary pavilions in an abstract planar sensibility for exhibitions in Norway and on the Continent.

After the war, construction resumed on Arneberg and Poulsson's Oslo City Hall and it was completed in 1951. Executed in large handmade red bricks with stone detailing, the massive cubic form with its two towers has a powerful presence on the Oslo waterfront (*see* Fig. 6.11). It also has an extensive public art programme, with numerous sculptures on the exterior and a large mural by Henrik Sørensen in the hall used for the Nobel awards.

The creation of a rhythmic architecture with an expressive formal order resulted in a Norwegian brutalism as expressed in the brick and concrete buildings of Kjell Lund and Nils Slaatto. The St Hallvard Church (1966) (Fig. 5.11), with its concave rounded concrete ceiling reminiscent of Le Corbusier's chapel at Ronchamp, France and the concrete frame and brick-infilled Chateau Neuf' Student Union (1971) are exemplary. Erling Viksjø's Oslo government building (1959) is an expressive concrete high-rise. The red brick and copper Sociological Institute (1960) in Oslo by Molle and Per Cappelen, Trond Eliassen and Birger Lambertz-Nilssen exhibits cultivated Aaltoesque qualities.

Sverre Fehn's early work exhibits a rationalist Miesian quality seen in two works that are horizontal expressions realized in concrete and glass: with Geir Grung he executed the Maihaugen Museum (1959) and the Økern nursing and seniors home (1955) in Oslo. Grung, with Georg Greve, designed the Vettre School (1958) in Asker, a comparable horizontal work in concrete and glass.

But Fehn's more personal expressive direction emerges in the Norwegian Pavilion for the 1958 World's Fair in Brussels and Nordic Pavilion at the Venice Biennale (1962). The Biennale pavilion, which

Fig. 5.12 The ruin of the medieval manor of the Archbishop of Hamar regains life in Sverre Fehn's museum restoration (1970). In the background is Lund and Slaatto's glass 'cathedral' (1998) covering the eleventh-century ruins of the Hamar Romanesque cathedral (*see* Fig. 6.12). (Photo: Author)

is still in use, is a quiet, yet dramatic essay in exposed crisscrossing concrete beams and girders filtering the bright Mediterranean light penetrating it. The Archbishopric Museum (1970) in Hamar is a vibrant synthesis of rational planning and material palpability, transforming modernism into a personal, experiential and expressive architecture (Fig. 5.12). Here Fehn leads one on an articulated journey – defined by a concrete pathway – over and through the medieval ruin: one is in constant tension between the experiences of new and old, tactile and smooth, open and closed and dark and light. The new concrete walkway winds through the existing building spaces while glazing panels are discreetly attached to the openings in the ruin's existing rubble walls. The new roof is supported by wooden trusses referencing medieval construction.

During this period a number of churches were built in Norway and many were brutalist-inspired works. These include Jan Inge Hovig's dynamic white concrete Arctic Church (1965) in Tromsø (Fig. 5.13); the expressive white concrete Kirkelandet Church (1964) in Kristiansund by Odd Østbye; and Hille Melbye Arkitekter's red brick Lambertseter Church

(1966) in Oslo. The red brick Åssiden Church (1967) in Drammen, with its grain-elevator-like cylindrical sanctuary, and the austere exposed concrete and glass Snarøya Church (1968) in Bærum are both by Odd Østbye and Harald Hille. A more traditional response is the wooden 'A' frame or boathouse-form church (1965) in Brumunddal by Molle and Per Cappelen.

The first large Norwegian satellite new town with a town centre, neighbourhood units and a tram connection to Oslo was Lambertseter (1951–62), by Frode Rinnan. Like other Nordic new town developments, a number of architects designed the residential areas. 'Skjetten Town' (late 1960s) in Skedsmo, east of Oslo, was one of the most ambitious low-rise high-density housing projects in post-war Scandinavia. The memorable red-painted wood Skjetten housing system, with its emphasis on modular prefabrication, flexibility and adaptability represents an interesting response to contemporaneous Norwegian housing and its social, political and architectural challenges. Designed by Resen, Throne-Holst and Hultberg with Nils-Ole Lund, the complex included about 1,500 housing units and social and commercial facilities.

Fig. 5.13 Jan Inge Hovig's white concrete Arctic Cathedral (1965) in Tromsø illustrates the dramatic atmosphere or mood captured when the midnight sun penetrates through the sanctuary, playing on the surfaces of the nested sloped roof form. (Photo: By Molde20 (Own work) [CC BY-SA 3.0 (http://creativecommons.org/licenses/by-sa/3.0)], via Wikimedia Commons)

Finland

Combining sensitively sited buildings executed in a material palette of brick, concrete, copper and wood, the Finns created a subtle and responsive modernism in the post-war period. As yellow brick is associated with pre- and post-war Danish architecture, in post-war Finland it was red brick; initially due to building material shortages but then coupled with being allied to Alvar Aalto's work in the 1950s.

Finnish new towns and post-war housing estates – especially Tapiola Garden City (1949 onwards) planned by Otto-I Meurman – embraced the Finns' enthusiasm for living close to nature. Tapiola was comprised of neighbourhoods separated by green zones and grouped around Aarne Ervi's Town Centre (1961) with its administrative building (*see* Fig. 6.16) and shopping facilities and the later addition of his recreational facility (1965). The housing complexes at Tapiola were designed by Finland's most important architects, including Viljo Revell, Kaija and Heikki Siren, Reima and Raili Pietilä and Aulis Blomstedt, among many others.

Alvar Aalto entered into his most creative and productive period following the war. Aino Aalto died in 1949 from cancer and Alvar married architect Elissa Mäkiniemi in 1952. The initial work of this period was in red brick, but by the late 1950s his material palette expanded. Of his red brick buildings the Säynätsalo Town Hall (1952) is without peer (Fig. 5.14). Aalto succeeded in placing the small civic complex in the Finnish forest in a way that humanized and civilized the landscape in the manner he was writing about in the 1920s. The building creates a plaza space surrounded with the red brick forms rooting the complex to its site. Here resides the memory of a small square in a northern Italian village, as well as becoming a mnemonic device through its grass-surfaced plaza with fountain and vine-covered walls, recalling a forest meadow or farm courtyard. The rest of the complex comprises shops and a library which complements the civic functions celebrated by the tall, massive council chamber.

Works in Helsinki that were executed in brick include the Rautatalo office building (1955) with its sky-lit atrium and copper curtain wall; the Public

Fig. 5.14 The red brick Säynätsalo Town Hall (1952) captures Alvar Aalto's concept of creating architecture that humanized and civilized the landscape. (Photo: Author)

Pensions Institute building (1956) with its sky-lit interviewing area; the undulating, curved form of the House of Culture (1958); and the main classroom building, library and dormitory at the Institute of Technology at Otaniemi (1964–70, now the Helsinki University of Technology). Aalto also executed the Teachers' College (1957) in Jyväskylä in red brick. With the Vuoksenniska Church (1959) outside Imatra, executed in white concrete, Aalto's material palette began to change and expand. At this time his buildings also incorporated more expressive and complex forms and interior spaces. The Seinäjoki town centre complex (1958–69) (*see* Fig. 7.11), with its white concrete church and library and blue-tiled town hall and cream-tiled theatre, exemplifies this as does the marble-clad Finlandia Hall (1971) in Helsinki, while the Museum of Modern Art (1972, with Jean-Jacques Baruël) in Aalborg offers an essay in the use of distinctive skylights. Aalto's production at this time demonstrates his deserved reputation and continued international stature.

While he dominated perceptions of Finnish developments internationally, Finland was much more than Aalto. Aulis Blomstedt provided an alternative direction, focusing on simplifying and systematizing architecture. Three housing projects in Tapiola – the red brick Ketju and Kolmirinne housing complex (1954) with its chain housing and apartment buildings, the Karhunpojat apartment building (1957) and the white plastered Riistapolku housing blocks (1961) – demonstrate his interest in modularity and rationality. Influenced by Mies van der Rohe, Blomstedt's theoretical writings sought to objectify architecture and his Helsinki Workers' Institute (1959, an annexe to Gunnar Taucher's 1929 Adult Education Centre) rigorously focused upon simplicity, austerity and abstraction. In Blomstedt, Mies van der Rohe, modular thinking and modernism found a spokesman who had great influence on the coming generation of Finnish architects (*see* 'The Intellectual Dimension in Nordic Architectural Thought').

Through Blomstedt, other Finnish architects, especially younger ones, had a path to avoid or eschew Aalto's influence by creating rationalistic, uncompromising buildings. The work of Aarno Ruusuvuori demonstrates this form of extreme simplicity, for he created a number of powerful works in exposed raw concrete and refined detailing. The Hyvinkää Church (1961) is a split pyramidal form with a great skylight illuminating the exposed interior structure (Fig. 5.15), while the more expressive brutalist Huutoniemi Church (1964) in Vaasa and boxlike Tapiola Church (1965) have austere light-filled interiors. The Weilin & Göös Printing Works

Fig. 5.15
Constructed of white concrete, Aarno Ruusuvuori's simple but powerful Hyvinkää Church (1961) is a split pyramidal form creating a dramatic sky-lit sanctuary. (Photo: Author)

(1964 and 1966) in Espoo, with its aggressively expressed structure, the concrete Roihvuori School (1966) in Helsinki with its transparent and translucent glazing and the Mikkeli police station (1968) are important works by Ruusuvuori. Three other works in concrete show brutalist influences: Erikki Elomaa's elementally composed church (1967) in Järvenpää, Pekka Pitkänen's Holy Cross funeral chapel (1967) in Turku and Jaakko and Unto Rantanen's Marina Palace Hotel (1974) in Turku.

Erkki Huttunen executed one of the first post-war curtain-walled buildings in downtown Helsinki – the sophisticated triangular-plan Sokos department store (1952), with its hotel and roof terrace restaurant. Toivo Korhonen produced several curtain-walled educational facilities, including the Social University (1962, with Jaakko Laapotti) in Tampere with its refined detailing and the Munkkivuori Coeducational School (1960) in Helsinki. He also designed the Lauritsala Church (1969, also with Laapotti) in Lappeenranta, with its sweeping roof form. Other works expressing technical proficiency and rational planning include Osmo Sipari's Finnish-Russian School (1964) in Helsinki; Timo Penttilä's skilfully sited and elegant Helsinki City Theatre (1967); Erik Kråkström, Kirmo Mikkola and Juhani Pallasmaa's Swedish Secondary School (1967) in Helsinki; Erkki Kairamo and

Jorma Pankakoski's austere Hyrylä garrison heating plant (1968); Woldemar Baeckman's graceful Sibelius Museum (1968) in Turku; and Bertel Saario and Juha Leiviskä's Kouvola City Hall (1969). Kirmo Mikkola, Kristian Gullichsen and Juhani Pallasmaa, among others, created Miesian-inspired houses, often using austere modular, prefabricated construction systems (*see* Fig. 5.9) (*see* 'The Minimalist House: Glass, Steel or Wood and Little Else').

While Viljo Revell executed a number of housing projects in Tapiola using prefabricated and modular construction methods, he is best known for his curtain-walled commercial and civic buildings. The Teollisuuskeskus office building and Palace Hotel (1952, with Keijo Petäjä) is sited prominently on the Helsinki harbour, while the Hyvon textile factory (1955) in Hanko expresses the idea of technical excellence seen in American commercial architecture. The Helsinki police station (1962), a mixed-use complex (1962) in central Vaasa and the KOP office building (1962) in Turku are all examples of his rationalist design sensibilities, while the Vatiala funeral chapel (1961) in Tampere, with its powerful arched roof, is a more elemental and brutalist expression. Revell won the international competition for the city hall in Toronto, Canada (1958–66) with a bold design of two curved curtain-walled towers.

Fig. 5.16 The forest is brought into the sanctuary space of Kaija and Heikki Siren's elegantly simple red brick and wood chapel (1957) at the Technical Institute in Otaniemi. (Photo: By Jisis (Own work) [CC BY-SA 3.0 (http://creativecommons.org/licenses/by-sa/3.0) or GFDL (http://www.gnu.org/copyleft/fdl.html)], via Wikimedia Commons)

Kaija and Heikki Siren completed two important works in red brick before expanding their material vocabulary: the National Theatre addition (1954) with its refined planar red brick and curtain-wall façade and the exquisite intimate wood and red brick chapel (1957) at the Technical Institute in Otaniemi (Fig. 5.16). Their Orivesi Church (1961) is of white concrete, while the Ympyrätalo or 'Circle House' office building (1968) in Helsinki, executed in copper, demonstrates their mastery of contemporaneous international curtain-wall construction.

Several works that took a more organic approach include Yrjö Lindegren's undulating 'Serpent House' housing complex (1951) and Timo and Tuomo Suomalainen's unique Church in the Rock (1969)

Fig. 5.17 Carved into its granite site, Timo and Tuomo Suomalainen's Church of the Rock (1969) in Helsinki has a shallow copper dome that is sky-lit around the edges, creating an ethereal, floating sensation. (Photo: By Ralf Roletschek (talk) – Fahrradtechnik auf fahrradmonteur.de (Own work) [FAL or GFDL 1.2 (http://www.gnu.org/licenses/old-licenses/fdl-1.2.html)], via Wikimedia Commons)

Fig. 5.18 Reima and Raili Pietilä's powerful and sculptural Kaleva Church (1960) in Tampere has vertical curved wall forms that allow full-height glazing to illuminate the sanctuary. (Photo: Author)

(Fig. 5.17), both in Helsinki. The church was carved into the granite site and has a shallow copper dome that is sky-lit around its edges, providing an ethereal, floating sensation.

Between Aalto and Blomstedt were Reima and Raili Pietilä, a husband-and-wife team, whose work appears organic but also explores the identity of place and Finnishness. While Reima executed the Finnish Pavilion at the 1958 Brussels World Fair, the two produced three exceptional buildings during this period. The vertically expressive Kaleva Church (1960) in Tampere has curved concrete and tile forms allowing light to penetrate between them (Fig. 5.18). Integrated into what appears a rock moraine is the Dipoli Student Union (1966) at the Technical Institute in Otaniemi, with its cave-like flowing roof form and forest-inspired vertical window mullions. The Suvikumpu residential area (1969) in Tapiola demonstrated the Pietiläs' ability to integrate a multi-storey apartment building into a forested site.

Modernism was able to maintain a lively presence in the North due to support from the four welfare state governments and the competency and expressiveness of Nordic architects. For the quarter-century following the Second World War, Scandinavian architects explored modernism through the lens of culturally relevant forms based upon regional and traditional characteristics. At the same time, they expanded their range of expression through incorporating sources of inspiration from the Continent, North America and Japan. Coupled with the forceful personalities of a number of internationally recognized practitioners, a younger group of architects was emerging who would have significant influence in the last quarter of the twentieth century and on into the twenty-first.

Chapter 6

NO LONGER YOUR PARENTS' MODERNISM: INTERNATIONAL INFLUENCES AND NORDIC IDENTITY (1970–2000)

Embracing Internationalism

T HE LAST QUARTER OF THE TWENTIETH century was a dynamic period for Nordic architects, both within Scandinavia and internationally. While the legacy modernists were in the twilight of their practices the next generation was in full stride. In the 1970s and 1980s there emerged a number of architects who pushed the boundaries of modernism and were interested in international trends. Like their predecessors these architects created distinctive practices that produced works that were immediately associated with them. The works produced by these practitioners continued to explore culturally relevant forms rooted in regional traditions, while expanding the expressive and material language of post-war modernism. As architectural activity increased worldwide, Nordic architects became active in exporting their ideas on form, space and materials internationally.

During the 1970s and 1980s modernism was undergoing critical assessment globally and some Scandinavian architects showed interest in international trends. 'Postmodernism' emerged, to propose an architecture having multiple meanings created through using historical references and associations, as opposed to the rational and abstract character of modernism. Internationally, postmodernism appeared to provided architects with a heightened sense of freedom in their search for form and meaning. Popular in North America, Japan and on the Continent, postmodernism embraced historicism

and used clever ironic and whimsical historic architectural quotations, decoration and ornamentation, while including vernacular sources for inspiration as well as high style ones.[38] Though Nordic architects seldom embraced the historicism of postmodernism, it did influence their architecture and was absorbed differently in each country.

But postmodernism was not the only critical trend emerging in architecture. In reaction to postmodernism, 'deconstructivism' emerged as a critique of the rationalism of modernism and historicism of postmodernism. While postmodernism embraced the historical references that modernism had shunned, deconstructivism rejected the postmodern acceptance of such literal allusions. Deconstructivist architecture is characterized by fragmentation, irregularity, unpredictability, complicated geometries and using non-rectilinear shapes to distort the envelope and form of a building.[39] At times the works recall early twentieth-century Russian constructivist architecture, especially their exaggerated paper projects of the 1920s. While Scandinavian architects did not always acknowledge the influence of deconstructivism on their work, as compared to its international popularity, some Nordic architecture of the 1990s incorporated constructivist organizational strategies and forms of expression.

At this time what held more intellectual sway in the North were the phenomenological architectural concepts introduced by the Norwegian architect and theorist Christian Norberg-Schulz and the concept of 'critical regionalism' formulated by the

British-American architectural educator Kenneth Frampton.[40] Internationally, Norberg-Schulz brought Martin Heidegger's ideas on 'dwelling' to architectural discourse, along with his own concept of *genius loci* – the importance of the 'spirit of place' (*see* 'The Intellectual Dimension of Nordic Architectural Thought'). At the same time, critical regionalism focused on the importance of a building being responsive to its surroundings, or place, coupled with local cultural and material influences. Frampton uses several Scandinavian architects as examples in explaining critical regionalism. Given the traditions and directions of Nordic architecture from the late nineteenth century on, these two intellectual trends held important currency.

In addition to interest in international architectural debates, Scandinavian architects embraced the increased importance of preservation and conservation of historic buildings, complexes and residential neighbourhoods as was occurring on the Continent and in North America. The oil crisis of the mid-1970s highlighted the importance of energy issues in building and focused awareness on larger environmental concerns. Residential areas and housing design began to transform, moving away from large-scale blocks to more integrated complexes fostering social interaction and contact, with diversity in the size and types of housing units, the inclusion of more social facilities and services and more varied architectural expression.

Modernism also maintained its coinage as a 'second' or neo-modernism emerged; an architecture based upon minimalist aesthetics and a sophisticated use of glass and metal. Influenced by the international architectural trends of the 1970s and 1980s, another generation of architects and architectural firms have emerged in the 1990s to continue to push the expressive boundaries of modernism. One change occurring in Nordic architectural practice was the growing number of larger architectural firms; firms that were active in their own country, the other Nordic countries and increasingly engaged internationally. All in all, the last quarter of the twentieth century was a period of an increasing openness in architectural exploration, setting the stage for the twenty-first.

Sweden

Important urban transportation facilities impacted Stockholm during the 1970s; a series of new underground or subway stations, called 'grotto stations', were built. The soft curving forms of these stations were complemented with public arts projects. Three stations in particular, the Stadion station (1973), the Technical University station (1973) and the Rådhuset or City Hall station (1975), have engaging and sophisticated artworks. It is well worth the time to travel the subway and enjoy the stations and artworks. The Vasa Terminal central bus station (1989) designed by the consortium Arkitektkontoren AET HB is not only a major transportation hub, but also a large and significant office and multi-use complex. An important civic work in Stockholm was the Parliament building reconstruction and addition of a new main chamber on the upper portion of the complex (1983) by Ahlgren Olsson Silow Arkitektkontor. Around the corner from Peter Celsing's cultural centre at Sergels Torg is his National Bank of Sweden (1976), with its thick rough-hewn dark granite slabs reminiscent of Renaissance rustication.

Carl Nyrén's work took several paths: the first is exemplified by a rational technical architecture as witnessed in the articulated prefabricated concrete system of the Arrhenius Laboratory (1970) at Stockholm University, the green steel and glass Sparbanken (1975) in Stockholm (Fig. 6.1) and the Pharmacia office and laboratory complex (1970–85) in Uppsala. At the same time he combines traditional tectonics with contextual responsiveness as seen in three wooden churches: the Ålidhem Church (1973) in Umeå, the Immanuel Church (1976) in Jönköping and the Gottsunda Church (1980) in Uppsala. Several Nyrén works have postmodern qualities: the striped red and black brick Uppsala public library (1986), the cubic red brick Halmstads Town Hall (1982) and the

Fig. 6.1 Carl Nyrén's green steel and glass Sparbanken (1975) in Stockholm exemplifies a more expressive rational technical architecture with its inward-stepped façade and expressive articulated structure. (Photo: By Holger.Ellgaard (Own work) [CC BY-SA 3.0 (http://creativecommons.org/licenses/by-sa/3.0)], via Wikimedia Commons)

orange-painted concrete County Museum (1992) in Jönköping with its roof of curved skylights.

Works using traditional tectonics and displaying vernacular imagery include Jan Gezelius and Gunnar Mattsson's National Museum of Ethnography (1978), which incorporates a wooden exterior finished with traditional Falun red paint, and Mattsson's Leksand cultural centre (1985), with its expressive use of wood and dynamic library space. An important work in Stockholm, the Vasa Museum (1990) by Marianne Dahlbäck and Göran Månsson, combines traditional materials with an expressive exterior form that includes ship masts (Fig. 6.2). The museum is concrete, with wooden panels painted in blue, '*falu svart*' or tar black, Falun red, yellow ochre and dark green.

Rosenberg & Steel Arkitektkontor's refined glass and steel swimming and sports complex (1973) in Sollentuna exemplifies neo-modern technical expression. Klas Anshelm's Kunsthall (1976) in Malmö is

a building about light and art, where a symphony of roof forms light the spaces. Noteworthy are the gallery skylights composed of a honeycombed structure providing shadowless light for the art. The two elegant glass and aluminium Gothia towers (1984) in Gothenburg by White Arkitekter include the Hotel Gothia with postmodern interior spaces. White's Oslo Plaza tower (1989) is a refined statement in glass and metal.

Ralph Erskine executed three important buildings at the Stockholm University campus at Frescati: the 'Allhouse' or student union (1981), the library (1982) and the sports hall (1983). The 'Allhouse', a seemingly irregularly planned building integrated into a hillside, is the more spatially and formally expressive of the three. The library is organized by a multi-storey 'book street' binding the interior spaces together, while elementally expressing programmatic functions on the exterior. The sports

Fig. 6.2 The colourful Vasa Museum (1990) in Stockholm, by Marianne Dahlbäck and Göran Månsson, combines traditional materials and colours with a dramatic form incorporating ships' masts. The museum displays the salvaged Swedish warship *Vasa* that sank in Stockholm harbour in 1628. (Photo: By Holger.Ellgaard (Own work) [CC BY-SA 3.0 (http://creativecommons.org/licenses/by-sa/3.0)], via Wikimedia Commons)

hall is a large open space created with curved glue-laminated beams and a multicoloured corrugated sheet metal roof. All Erskine's Swedish housing projects were influenced by his iconic sinuous, colourful brick Byker Wall (1969–81) housing complex in Newcastle-on-Tyne (UK): the Nya Bruket (1978) in Sandviken, Myrstuguberget (1986) in Vårby and Ekerö Centre (1991) outside Stockholm. The spectacular Lilla Bommen office building (1990, with White Arkitekter) is a dominant landmark in central Gothenburg (Fig. 6.3).

Swedish housing developments not only became more expressive than the earlier large-scale block estates, but exhibited more diversity in the types of housing options offered, the material palettes used and the inclusion of social services and facilities. Kista (1980) in Stockholm by Höjer and Ljungqvist Arkitektkontor was among the first of these new complexes. Notable examples include the red brick Erskine-esque Warm Front blocks (1987) at Skarpnäcks by Arken Arkitekter and the postmodern Minneberg (1987) by

Brunnberggruppèn Arkitekter, both in Stockholm; White Arkitekter's Erskine-influenced 'Mjölnaren' neighbourhood (1984) in Gothenburg; and the concrete and brick Södra Hägernäs (1985) in Täby by Engstrand and Speek. The residential-scaled Grimsta By small house area (1979) in Upplands Väsby by Brunnberggruppèn Arkitekter and the intimate village-like Klitterbyn vacation house area (1978) in Ängelholm by Landskronagruppen provided alternative housing paradigms.

Johan Celsing's Millesgården Art Gallery (1999), on the island of Lidingö outside Stockholm, is a refined work in stone, glass and wood, while the library of the School of Business, Economics and Law (1995) in Gothenburg by Erséus, Frenning & Sjögren Arkitekter, has a three-storey sky-lit atrium and dynamic auditorium space. Stintzing Arkitektur's evocative graphic arts school (1991) in Tumba outside Stockholm, with its leaning walls and inclined columns, is as close as Sweden gets to deconstructivism.

Fig. 6.3 The expressive vertical form of Ralph Erskine's Lilla Bommen office building (1990, with White Arkitekter) makes it a dominant landmark in central Gothenburg. (Photo: By Arild Vågen (Own work) [CC BY-SA 4.0 (http://creativecommons.org/licenses/by-sa/4.0)], via Wikimedia Commons)

Three works by foreign architects indicate the growing interest of the international community in working in Scandinavia, a situation that increases in the twentieth-first century. The Dutch Benedictine monk and architect Hans van der Laan executed the austere Benedictine Abbey (1995) in Mariavall, in a modest palette of concrete, concrete blocks and untreated wood planks. Located on Skeppsholmen

Island in Stockholm are Spanish architect Rafael Moneo's refined white modernist Architecture and Design Centre (1998) and red brick Museum of Modern Art (1998) with its elegant pyramidal skylights.

Denmark

Jørn Utzon's iconic Bagsværd Church (1976) houses a dramatic, spatially exuberant cloud-like ceiling within a seemingly modest industrial building form; here sky, earth and the individual are brought together in a powerful experience (Fig. 6.5). The sanctuary capitalizes on its white curved form to maximize the quality and quantity of light, allowing the time of day and weather conditions to animate and activate the sanctuary. The complex is organized around a series of courtyard spaces, while the exterior is executed in white prefabricated concrete and white glazed panels. The Paustian furniture store (1987) in Copenhagen has a light-filled exhibition atrium with column forms inspired by beech forests. Utzon's Skagen Odde Nature Centre (1989, with Jan Utzon) is an enclosed compound incorporating courtyard spaces and square glass and concrete pavilions with pyramidal roofs and periscope-like skylights.

Brutalism continued in Denmark, as seen in works by Friis and Moltke. The well-crafted concrete Vestervang housing complex (1970) in Aarhus and sophisticated concrete and brick Odder Town Hall (1972, with H.P. Holm) are exemplary. Their light-filled secondary schools in red brick have animated concrete structures and daylight-gathering roof forms: Skanderborg (1973), Viborg (1974), Langkær (1974) in Tilst and Silkeborg (1977) typify this. The expressive elementally composed Ellevang Church (1974) and Skjoldhøj Church (1984), both in Aarhus suburbs, are of white concrete.

Other brutalist-inspired works include Kjær & Richter's red brick and concrete Danish School of Journalism (1973) in Aarhus and Vilhelm Wohlert's orderly red brick Danish Technological Institute

The Rudolf Steiner Seminary in Järna, Sweden, is an anthroposophist educational and healing institution. Austrian-born artist and scientist Rudolf Steiner developed the 'spiritual science' of anthroposophy. For Steiner this was a path of knowledge aiming to guide the spiritual element in the human to the spiritual in the universe. He saw all natural phenomena as interconnected spiritually and dependent upon a larger whole. The designs at Järna are influenced by the architectural ideas and designs of Steiner, particularly his early twentieth-century buildings in Switzerland – the First (1919) and Second (1928) Goetheanum. Influenced by Goethe's theory of metamorphosis, Steiner accepts the notion in Goetheanistic architecture that a building should relate to its site, its time, its building material and its function. Here, function includes a larger sense of atmosphere expressed through the architecture.

Danish architect Erik Asmussen's complex at Järna articulates the integrative and holistic ideals of Steiner's anthroposophy. Designed over a number of years beginning in 1966, the complex forms a village-like setting with over twenty buildings including a clinic, performance arts centre, educational centre, farm and market garden, mill, bakery and housing. Asmussen's designs are tactile, intuitive, alive, organic and ordered, yet contemporary. The buildings form a distinctive and idiosyncratic ensemble with unique spaces and forms referencing nature and traditional architecture. Together with the landscape design, which is both cultivated and natural, the complex provides a unified sense of well-being.[41]

The social and cultural focus of the seminary is the Culture House (1992), an expression of art, craft, spirituality and functionality (Fig. 6.4). It is a most intriguing form, as the structure embodies Steiner's view that form must derive from the nature of the activities it houses. The building is an assemblage of masses, each defining a separate function or space. The largest volume in the composition expresses its function as auditorium, the most important space within the building. The blue external walls curve gently to meet the black roofs, with windows and skylights illuminating the activities within.

Other works influenced by Asmussen and the Steiner philosophy are the Steiner School Kindergarten (1981) in Bergen by Arbeidsgruppen Hus and the Mikonkari Recreational Centre (1986) by Anna and Lauri Louekari and Kaarlo Viljanen in Raahe, Finland.

Fig. 6.4 The Culture House (1992) at the Rudolph Steiner Seminary in Järna, Sweden, by Danish architect Erik Asmussen, is a most intriguing form as it embodies Steiner's view that form must derive from the nature of the activities within the building. (Photo: 'Kulturhuset i Ytterjärna Södertälje'. Licensed under CC BY-SA 3.0 via Wikimedia Commons - https://commons.wikimedia.org/wiki/File:Kulturhuset_i_Ytterj%C3%A4rna_S%C3%B6dert%C3%A4lje.jpg#/media/File:Kulturhuset_i_Ytterj%C3%A4rna_S%C3%B6dert%C3%A4lje.jpg)

Fig. 6.5 The sanctuary of Jorn Utzon's iconic Bagsværd Church (1976) in Copenhagen capitalizes on its curved billowing white cloud-like concrete forms to maximize the quality and quantity of light within the space; this allows the time of day and weather conditions to animate and activate the space. (Photo: Krysta Mae Dimick).

(1975) in Copenhagen. Copenhagen's Panum Institute (1975), by Eva and Nils Koppel, Gert Edstrand and Poul Erik Thyrring, is a large expressive brick and concrete teaching complex. Knut Munk's forceful Grieg Hall (1978) in Bergen has a concrete concert hall embedded in a CorTen steel and glass lobby space. Halldor Gunnløgsson and Jørn Nielsen's red brick Gammel Holte Church (1978) in Rudersdal and Dall and Lindhardsten's large red brick town hall and library complex (1986) in Holstebro, with its undulating walls and well-composed fenestration patterns, are also indebted to brutalism.

Inger and Johannes Exner executed numerous brutalist-influenced churches with refined detailing and unique bell towers. The Islev Church (1970) in Copenhagen has detailing reminiscent of Sigurd Lewerentz's brick churches; in Aalborg the Gug Church (1972) incorporates brutalist concrete work while the Nørre Uttrup Church (1977) has a beautiful red brick sanctuary; and the Sædden Church (1978) in Esbjerg has an undulating brick sanctuary space. In the 1990s, while their red brick churches become more formally and spatially expressive the sanctuary spaces were now executed in white, as seen in the Verklund Church (1994), the Skæring Church (1994) in Aarhus and the Ølby Church (1997).

Dissing + Weitling took over Arne Jacobsen's office upon his death in 1971, completed his unfinished projects and emerging as a force in Danish architecture. A number of their important works were international, while they carried on Jacobsen's concern for expressive yet refined, well-detailed buildings. Their Sonofon headquarters (1999) in Copenhagen points to the neo-modernism prevalent in Danish architecture. Other neo-modern works include Ole Meyer's Belle Centre (1975) in Copenhagen, an expansive conference and exhibition complex executed in metal and glass; Krohn & Hartvig Rasmussen's refined steel and glass University centre (1978) in Odense; and Kjær & Richter's Aarhus Concert Hall (1982) (Fig. 6.6) with its elegant glass and metal lobby.

Henning Larsen's Gentofte Central Library (1985) is a modernist essay in whiteness reminiscent of the 1930s, while his sophisticatedly planned Copenhagen Business School (1989) celebrates circulation with a white light-filled interior street accented by blue and pink transition spaces. In the 1990s Larsen's work assumed the mantra of neo-modernism: the glass and perforated metal panelled *BT* newspaper building (1993) and the refined multi-building Nordea headquarters (1999) (Fig. 6.7) are both in Copenhagen. The Mærsk McKinney Møller Institute (1999) at

Fig. 6.6 Kjær & Richter's elegant glass and steel lobby of the Aarhus Concert Hall (1982) provides a dramatic stage for the comings and goings of the evening concertgoers. (Photo: By EHRENBERG Kommunikation (Aarhus musichouse) [CC BY-SA 2.0 (http://creativecommons.org/licenses/by-sa/2.0)], via Wikimedia Commons)

the University of Southern Denmark in Odense and the Malmö City Library (1999) are elemental compositions executed in masonry and glass. A unique creation is the cubic white concrete Enghøj Church (1994) in Randers with its cleft roof and sloping wooden ceiling.

The impact of preservation and adaptive use of historic buildings can be witnessed in Hertz and Thomsen's adaptation of an 1805 warehouse into the Nyhavn Hotel (1971) and Box 25's Young People's House (1972); both are progressive urban interventions within Copenhagen's historic fabric. Inger and Johannes Exner executed two major restoration projects: Koldinghus Castle (1972–92) with elegant new wooden columns and vaulting contrasting the original massive brick structure, and Copenhagen's iconic

Fig. 6.7 Henning Larsen's multi-building Nordea headquarters (1999) in Copenhagen is an essay in neo-modernism, with its rationalized forms and refined metal and glass detailing. It sits across the waterway from the 'Black Diamond' or Royal Library extension (see Fig. 6.9). (Photo: Krysta Mae Dimick)

Rundetårn and Trinity Church (1983) – the seventeenth-century observation tower has an impressive equestrian staircase.

While the Farum Centre Point (1974) housing complex designed by Viggo Møller-Jensen, and Bente Aude and Boje Lundgaard's 'Sjølund' cluster houses (1978) in Helsingør demonstrated the interest in more humane and nuanced housing projects, it is in housing where postmodern influence is seen in Denmark. Two complexes built for the Blangstedgård Housing Exhibition (1988) in Odense – Poul Ingemann's Plot 15 and 3XNielsen's Plot 12 – have postmodernism's cultivated historicist imagery. In particular, Ingemann's Plot 15 explicitly referenced Danish 1920s classicism with temple-like façades and mannered columnar elements.

Høje Tåstrup new town (1988), by Jacob Blegvad Arkitektkontor, incorporates postmodern axial and hierarchical classical planning principles while using brick as the primary material for its neo-traditional buildings, while a mix of postmodern ideas and machine imagery combine in Arkitektgruppen Aarhus's Damhusengen housing (1990) in Rødovre. But it is Knut Munk's Tycho Brahe planetarium (1989) in Copenhagen, with its yellow slope-topped cylindrical form accented in blue zigzag tiles, the whole sitting on a striped masonry base, that captures postmodernism's flair (Fig. 6.8).

Tegnestuen Vandknutsen achieved several innovative housing complexes: their two-phase vernacular-influenced Herfølge housing complex (1971–84, with Karsten Vibild), south of Køge, and their Blue Corner housing intervention (1989) which creatively incorporates the urban site's existing buildings in the Christianshaven district of Copenhagen. Several collective housing projects reuse and adapt existing buildings: Tegnestuen Vandknutsen's spatially interesting Jystrup Savværk or sawmill housing cooperative (1984) has an internal street and communal facilities, while Jan Gudmand-Høyer and Jes Edwards transformed the Jernstøberiet or iron foundry building near Roskilde into cooperative housing (1980).

Schmidt, Hammer & Lassen's animated and evocative 'Black Diamond' or Royal Library extension (1999) (Fig. 6.9) sits on a Copenhagen waterway; its polished black granite multi-angled façade houses a gracious sky-lit central atrium. Søren Robert Lund's ARKEN Museum of Modern Art (1993, with Vilhelm

Fig. 6.8 The Tycho Brahe planetarium (1989) in Copenhagen, by Knut Munk, captures postmodernism's flair, with its yellow slope-topped cylindrical form finished in zigzag blue tiles. (Photo: By Albertyanks – Albert Jankowski (Own work) [Public domain], via Wikimedia Commons)

Fig. 6.9 Schmidt, Hammer & Lassen's 'Black Diamond' or extension to the Royal Library (1999) in Copenhagen is an evocative polished granite and glass multi-angled volume. It sits across the waterway from the Nordea headquarters *(see Fig. 6.7)*. (Photo: Author)

Lauritzens Tegnestue) in Ishøj, south of Copenhagen, embraces the organizational and formal strategies of deconstructivism, from its fractured, intersecting spatial elements to its elaborated, sharp forms colliding together. Few buildings in Scandinavia embrace deconstructivism with the energy that ARKEN exhibits.

Norway

As with her Nordic cousins, Norway's architects not only expanded design directions formed in the post-war era, but became very interested in international trends, particularly postmodernism, while also embracing the neo-modernism emerging throughout Scandinavia. Towards the end of the century important large urban developments were occurring in Oslo and elsewhere due to increased oil revenues that enhanced both economic growth and development in Norway.

The rough-cast concrete and glass Bryggens Museum (1976) in Bergen by Øivind Maurseth exemplifies brutalist civic architecture, while the Østerås Church (1974) in Bærum by Viggo Kippenes and Ashish Krishna, like numerous Norwegian churches, incorporates brutalism's red brick and concrete materiality. Harald Hille's churches combine the red brick influence of brutalism with expressive bell towers: the pitched-roof Strovner Church (1979) and Furuset Church (1980), both in Oslo, and the Helgerud Church (1982) in Bærum. A later example of brutalist inspiration is NWS's brick and concrete Kongsberg Town Hall (1993), an addition to the town's historic church. The brick volumes of Eliassen and Lambertz-Nilssen's Norwegian Maritime Museum (1973) and Sandefjord Town Hall (1975) exhibit robust yet cultivated Aaltoesque qualities.

This was a period of church building throughout Norway and many were very traditional and referential in execution, incorporating wood construction and steeply pitched roofs. An exemplary one in this idiom is Aksel Fronth's red wooden Fjellhamar Church (1989) in Lørenskog. To see the expressive range of religious architecture at this time we can turn to the concrete and sweeping copper-roofed Slettebakken Church (1970) in Bergen by Tore Sveram; the expressive modernist-inspired white concrete Sinsen Church (1971) in Oslo by Turid and Kristen Bernhoff Evensen; Nils Henrik Eggen's white concrete and metal-roofed Kolstad Church (1986) in Trondheim;

Architectural theory has not necessarily played an active role in modern and contemporary Nordic architectural practice. Granted, numerous Functionalist architects wrote essays and critiques of the new modern architecture for newspapers and popular magazines. But interest in architectural theory did emerge and have influence on architectural thinking. Gregor Paulsson, an art historian, wrote the highly publicized propaganda piece *Vakrare vardagsvara* ('More Beautiful Everyday Objects') in 1919 for the Swedish Society, which promoted beauty and thoughtful design in industrially produced objects. Paulsson was also Commissioner General for the 1930 Stockholm Exhibition and, in concert with Sven Markelius, Uno Åhrén, Gunnar Asplund, Eskil Sundahl and Wolter Gahn, produced *acceptera* in 1931; Nordic modernism's one manifesto demanded that

Functionalism must be accepted and embraced.

In Finland there was Aulis Blomstedt; without question the foremost theoretician in Finnish architecture during the post-war period. Influenced by the work of Mies van der Rohe, Blomstedt sought to develop an objective theory of architecture that could be verified through practice, with simplicity, austerity and abstraction as the essence. He focused on clarifying architecture through intellectual speculations which were published in *Le Carré Bleu*, the legendary theoretical periodical he co-founded in 1958. Modular and proportional discipline formed his foundation, as he sought to develop a universal system derived from human measurements and dimensional harmony. The crystallization of his research was *Canon 60* (1961), a system of dimensions and proportions in which the

principles of mathematical and musical harmony were applied to building, bringing the principles of harmonic proportions into current practice.

Though an active architect and educator, Christian Norberg-Schulz became internationally recognized for his influential theoretical and historical writings: *Intentions in Architecture* (1965), *Existence, Space and Architecture* (1971), *Meaning in Western Architecture* (1975), *Genius Loci: Towards a Phenomenology of Architecture* (1979) and *The Concept of Dwelling* (1984), among his many works, were central contributions to architectural thought. His theoretical work saw a shift from an initial focus on analytical and psychological concerns to the issues of phenomenology of place. He was among the first architectural theorists to bring the thinking of Martin Heidegger

and Lund and Slaatto's refined concrete vaulted St Magnus Church (1988) in Lillestrøm.

During this time Sverre Fehn produced his most poignant architectural works – works articulating the interaction between nature and architecture and place and materials. The concrete Glacier Museum in Fjærland (1991) marks its presence in the landscape by appearing to have been left as a glacier receded (Fig. 6.10). The roof is accessible for panoramic viewing of the surrounding glaciers, while a

crystalline glass element fractures the solid building mass. The Aukrust Museum (1996) in Alvdal, housing the work of artist Kjell Aukrust, is a linear concrete and slate form with refined wood interior detailing. Celebrating the work of poet and linguist Ivar Aasen, the Aasen Centre (2000) in Ørsta, which is embedded into its hillside site, is an essay in concrete with elegant wood trim and accents. Fehn was the first Scandinavian architect to receive the prestigious Pritzker Prize in architecture (1997), to the field, particularly his notion of 'dwelling'. To dwell is essential and vital to humans; dwelling establishes a meaningful relationship between the individual and place. Place identification gives our life presence and identity. For Norberg-Schulz, the writings of phenomenologists Gaston Bachelard, Maurice Merleau-Ponty and Martin Heidegger provide understandings to the structure of place and human interaction within that world. Using Norwegian, Italian and North African settings, he examined the qualitative conditions of place and the constituent elements that inform the creation of a specific place. Places, built or natural, typically have a floor or ground – a ceiling, roof, or sky – and walls, trees, hills or other materials, forming spaces or enclosures. To dwell means to respect place and understand its essential elements and qualities; as sand is vital to desert dwellers and snow to those dwelling in the North. Architects must recognize the identity of a place and take

possession of it through manifesting its qualitative, unmeasurable aspects in their work.

An active architect, educator and theorist, Juhani Pallasmaa, like his mentor and teacher Aulis Blomstedt, balances practice and writing. Like Norberg-Schulz, his writings on phenomenology have played a vital role in architectural discourse. An important aspect of Pallasmaa's work focuses on the idea of 'multi-sensory architecture'; that is, architecture needs to be understood and experienced as multi-sensory phenomena: 'qualities of matter, space and scale are measured equally by the eye, ear, nose, skin, tongue, skeleton and muscle. Architecture strengthens ... one's sense of being in the world ...'.[42] Eschewing vision as the primary means of experiencing architecture, he calls for directly encountering a building; contending that architectural theory, criticism and education must return to the cultural foundation of architecture. Experiential and

sensual interaction with a work of architecture and its place in the world provide a more complete and existential understanding. His published books include *Eyes of the Skin: Architecture and the Senses* (1996), *The Architecture of Image: Existential Space in Cinema* (2001), *Encounters: Architectural Essays* (2001) and *Encounters 2: Architectural Essays* (2012); the latter two are compendiums of his many articles and essays for numerous international journals and presentations.

It is not inconsequential that the two major threads in modern and contemporary Nordic architectural thought centre on modernism's focus on rationality, abstraction and serial production of everyday objects and buildings and the experiential and phenomenological understanding of the essential role of place, culture and materiality in architecture. The tension between the two, a very creative one, not only defines Nordic architecture of the twentieth century but animates the architecture of the twenty-first.

the highest international honour an architect can achieve.[43]

The Miesian-influenced glass block and steel St Olav Church (1973) in Trondheim by Per Kartvedt embraces neo-modernism, as do three buildings at the Norwegian University of Science and Technology in Trondheim (NTNU): the glass and metal-panelled Gunnerus Science Library (1975) by Anne and Einar Myklebust; the Marine Technology Centre (1979) by Asplan Arkitekter; and the Elektro E building (1986)

with its glazed streets by Per Knudsen Arkitektkontor. Knudsen also executed the metal and glass OlavsKvartalet shopping mall and Olavshallen auditorium (1989), an intervention into the urban fabric of Trondheim. In Oslo examples of neo-modernism include 4B Arkitekter's symmetrical arrangement of red brick with copper and glass curtain wall for the Norwegian Theatre (1985); Lund and Slaatto's block square Nordic Bank (1987), with its combination of concrete, metal and glass curtain walls, and their large

Fig. 6.10 With glaciers on the surrounding mountains, the concrete Glacier Museum (1991) in Fjærland, by Sverre Fehn, appears to have been left in the landscape as the glaciers receded. (Photo: Author)

Kredittkassens headquarters (1978), with its renovated exterior and stunning sky-lit interior atrium. Hultberg, Resen, Thorne-Holst and Boguslawski's central transportation station (1987) in Oslo has a constructivist-influenced glass clock tower. Niels Torp executed three neo-modernist works: the Norwegian Data office (1985) in Oslo, the elegant white concrete and glass SAS headquarters (1990) in Stockholm and the elegant glazed-roofed Nils Erickson bus terminal (1996) in Gothenburg.

Postmodernism seemed to have more currency in Norway than other Nordic countries. Its major proponents, Jon Lundberg and Jan Digerud, were among the first to incorporate postmodernism's idea of creating historically associative and referential works. They produced a number of houses and house remodels in Oslo suburbs, including Digerud's own house (1972), using mannered, whimsical, vernacular and historicist elements. In Oslo these qualities were

also seen in their classicized addition to the Glasmagasinet department store (1974), the whimsical Tower Suite (1975) in the Grand Hotel, the highly pictorial university press offices (1982) influenced by the American architect Charles Moore and the whimsical historicist upper-storeys addition capping Henrik Bull's 1917 Hannevig office tower (1983) (Fig. 6.11), all in association with F.S. Platou.

In Oslo additional postmodern works include the red brick classically referenced offices at Akersgata 13 (1983) by F.S. Platou; the yellow brick Arkaden department store (1983) with whimsical entry and elements by Kjell Østlie, Sigmund Skeie and Arve Nyhus; and the striped brick apartment block (1992) at Motzfeldts Gate 21 by Asplan Arkitekter. In Trondheim the concrete Product Design department (1996) at NTNU Gløshaugen by Voll Arkitekter has a mannered columned portico with a metal cone-shaped entrance. Kirstin Jarmund Arkitekter's

Fig. 6.11 In this panorama of downtown Oslo and the Oslofjord taken from the Akershus fortress, from left to right there is the Aker Brygge mixed-use development (from 1982 on), with its adventurous admixture of styles; the monolithic red brick City Hall (1951) by Arneberg and Poulsson, with its twin towers; and Henrik Bull's thin white eight-storey mid-block Nordic classic Hannevig office building (1918), with the whimsical postmodern upper-storeys addition (1983) by Lundberg and Digerud. (Photo: 'Aker Brygge and Vika Panorama' by Daniel78 – Own work (Nikon D300). Licensed under CC BY-SA 2.5 via Wikimedia Commons)

expressive elementally articulated Stensby Kindergarten (1994) in Eidsvoll incorporates a pastel colour palette referencing the work of American architect Michael Graves.

Beginning in the late 1980s, major urban makeovers began occurring in Norway. One of the most impactful and significant was the transformation of the Oslo shipyards, near City Hall, into the Aker Brygge mixed-use district developed between 1982 and 1998 (Fig. 6.11). An adventurous admixture of styles, images and materials designed by Telje-Torp-Aasen Arkitektkontor (among others) and located along the Oslofjord, Aker Brygge contains shopping, restaurants and entertainment venues along with office space and housing. A significant work in the complex is Kari Nissen Brodtkorb's Beach residential and commercial complex (1990); this is a red brick and black-painted steel interpretation of nautical and warehouse images from the former shipyard.

Lund and Slaatto's expressive steel and glass 'Hamardomen' (1998) or 'cathedral' at the Hedmark Museum in Hamar protects the eleventh-century ruins of the Romanesque cathedral (Fig. 6.12), while their metal and glass Midgard Historical Centre (1999) in Borre, with its wooden hull-shaped entry canopy, houses Viking artefacts. Lunde and Løvseth

Fig. 6.12 Lund and Slaatto's expressive streel and glass 'cathedral' or 'Hamardomen' (1998) at the Hedmark Museum in Hamar protects the ruins of the Hamar Romanesque cathedral (also see Fig. 5.12). (Photo: Author)

Fig. 6.13 In the Olympic Art Museum (1994) in Lillehammer, Snøhetta created an evocative undulating wooden wall addition and glass connection to the original museum building. (Photo: Author)

executed the billowing glass and metal Tønsberg and Nøtterøy Library (1992) and the stone-clad Stavanger Petroleum Museum (1999), with its three metal and glass cylindrical forms recalling oil storage units.

The Oslo Spektrum (1990) by LPO Arkitektkontor is an indoor multi-purpose arena that is clad in tiles designed by artist Rolf Nesch, while F.S. Platou's office building at Schous Plass 8 (1990) in Oslo is an essay in refined black granite and glass. Two works in Hamar were produced for the 1994 Winter Olympics: Niels Torp's dynamic speed skating oval or 'Viking Ship' arena (1991, with Biong & Biong) and the Olympic Amphitheatre (1992) by Hultberg, Resen, Thorne-Holst and Boguslawski. Capturing the sense of appropriate Nordic construction traditions was one of the major public works of the decade, Oslo's new airport (1998) at Gardermoen by the architectural consortium Aviaplan. Also at the airport is Reiulf Ramstad Architects' restrained Customs and Excise building (1998), with its creative interior spatial organization.

At this time Snøhetta emerged as one of Norway's most innovative firms. Interested in the creative tension between architecture and landscape architecture, the Sonja Henie plaza (1989, with Alf Haukeland) and Olafia urban plaza, both in Oslo, demonstrate their crafting of site and creation of place as instrumental in their work. In the Lillehammer Olympic Art Museum (1994) (Fig. 6.13) with its evocative undulating wooden wall and glass connection to the original building and the artfully placed simple rectangular concrete tube of the Karmøy Fishing Museum (1998) the clarity of their concepts is seen.

Finland

Finnish architects examined a range of ideas, from expanding the modernist rationalism of Aulis Blomstedt, through experiential buildings manifesting culture, place and materiality, to work influenced

Fig. 6.14 The sanctuary of Juha Leiviskä's Myyrmäki Church (1984) in Vantaa is a light-filled space with expressive planar white-on-white layered walls. (Photo: Author)

brick St Thomas Church (1975) in Oulu, the linear yellow brick Myyrmäki Church (1984) in Vantaa (Fig. 6.14) and the red brick St John's or Männistö Church (1992) in Kuopio combine expressive parallel, layered, free-standing planes creating stunning daylight-filled white-on-white interior sanctuary spaces – spaces among the most elegant of this period.

Organized around a courtyard, Käpy and Simo Paavilainen's red brick Olari Church (1981) in Espoo has a dynamic white sanctuary, as does their postmodern-influenced St Michael Church and Parish Centre (1988) in Helsinki. The white brick Pirkkala Church (1994) in Tampere, which receives dramatic daylight patterns in the sanctuary, indicates their continued focus on dynamic interior spaces. The Munkkiniemi Health Centre (1992) and Stage 1 of the University of Vaasa (1994) are complexes organized along red brick circulation spines with white and glazed figural forms expressing their various programmatic functions.

Gullichsen, Kairamo and Vormala typify a firm where the principals are forceful designers with projects reflecting each individual's design inclinations. Kristian Gullichsen's red brick Malmi Church (1981) continues the culture of materials of postwar Finland, while the Kauniainen Church (1983) and Pieksämäki cultural centre (1989), both in white concrete recalling modernist works of the 1930s, illustrate his concept of building as wall to order the site, programme and form. Erkki Kairamo's work, influenced by Russian constructivism, includes the Marimekko textile works (1974) in Helsinki, the paper mill (1977) in Varkaus and the Itäkeskus commercial complex and office tower (1987), all essays in elemental constructivist expression, including metal and glass cladding and articulated building elements. These characteristics are playfully expressed in his Niittykumpu Fire Station (1991) in Espoo (Fig. 6.15). Timo Vormala's work is more traditional in its cultural and material expression; as seen in the Varistro apartment complex (1980) in Vantaa and the low-rise white clapboard Kyläauutarinpuisto housing estate (1985) in Helsinki. The firm's glazed curtain-wall

by international ideas and trends and finally to more personal individual expressions.

Several Finns explored the qualitative aspects of religious space, creating white-on-white interiors incorporating myriad interior lighting fixtures to recall starry winter skies, while using traditional exterior materials such as brick. The churches of Juha Leiviskä synthesize a dramatic Baroque-like use of natural light with the abstract compositional principles of Dutch *De Stijl* architecture of the 1920s. The parish centre (1970) for the Nakkila Church, the red

Fig. 6.15 The Niittykumpu fire station (1991) in Espoo is exemplary of the Russian constructivist influence found in Erkki Kairamo's architecture. (Photo: Author)

extension to Stockmann's department store (1989) reinterprets the rhythms of Frosterus's muscular 1930 brick building in a light and refined fashion.

Neo-modernism's importance is witnessed in Kaija and Heikki Siren's refined and polished granite-clad Graniittitalo office building (1982) in Helsinki; Matti Mäkinen and Kaarina Löfström's extensive Valio headquarters (1978) in Helsinki, with its rich and complex industrial imagery; Kari Virta's Oulu University Faculty of Technology complex (1975) with a concrete structure and colourful metal panels; Jan Söderlund and Evkki Valovirta's student village (1976) in Turku with its systematized modular construction system; Jaakko and Kaarina Laapotti's Rosendahl Hotel (1977) in Tampere and Kouvola Church (1978), both executed in metal with minimalist industrial expression; and Pitkänen, Laiho and Raunio's curved curtain-walled extension to the Parliament building (1978) in Helsinki. Two works in Oulu, the city theatre (1972) and library (1982), by Marjatta and Martti Jaatinen, are refined exercises in metal and glass.

Fig. 6.16 The refined Tapiola cultural centre (1989) in Espoo exemplifies Arto Sipinen's later more abstract work executed in white. Behind the centre is Arne Ervi's Tapiola administrative building (1961). (Photo: Author)

Arto Sipinen's earliest work included a series of red brick buildings influenced by Aalto on the University of Jyväskylä campus: the main library (1974), administration building (1974), music building (1976) and art building (1976). This Aaltoesque character also informs the Raisio (1981) and Kauhajoki (1983) Town Halls. Beginning in the 1980s, Sipinen's work assumes a white, abstract quality reminiscent of Le Corbusier's 1930s modernism and the work of American architect Richard Meier. His Imatra cultural centre and art museum (1986), the refined Tapiola cultural centre (1989) (Fig. 6.16), the expressive Mikkeli concert hall (1989) and the city halls in Tammela (1991) and Mäntsälän (1992) demonstrate this rigorous, sophisticated and elegant white modernism.

A decade hiatus in procuring work followed the Pietiläs' initial success. During this period Reima served as a professor of architecture at the University of Oulu and was influential in focusing the school on creating distinctive regional architecture. In the

Hervanta suburb of Tampere the recreational and parish centre (1978) and commercial market hall (1979) have a somewhat postmodern quality due to the materials and imagery used. The spirit of earlier works is evoked by the Lieksa Church (1982) built on the foundations of an Engel neoclassical church; 'Metso', the animated and vibrant main library (1986) in Tampere, and 'Mäntyniemi', the Finnish presidential residence (1993) outside Helsinki.

Focusing on creating a distinctive local and regional architecture, the work by Oulu School architects include a series of red brick buildings by Heikki Taskinen: the striking Törnävä funeral chapel and crematorium (1979) in Seinäjoki; the Pitkäkangas School (1983) in Oulunsalo, with battered walls and white and blue sheet metal concourse spaces; and the Deaconess Institute rehabilitation centre (1987) in Oulu. Organized around a courtyard, the red brick Oulunsalo Town Hall (1982) with tiled roofs and wooden trim, by Kari Niskasaari, Reijo Niskasaari,

Fig. 6.17 Nurmela, Raimoranta and Tasa's funky 'BePOP' commercial centre (1989) in Pori shows the whimsical and exaggerated character often seen in postmodern architecture. (Photo: Author)

Kaarlo Viljanen, Ilpo Väisänen and Jorma Öhman, is an iconic Oulu School work.

Postmodernism in Finland is best seen in the pseudo-classical references of Nurmela, Raimoranta, and Tasa's Malmi post office (1984), the amalgam of forms and images used in their Kuhmo library (1984), and the funky 'BePOP' commercial centre (1989) in Pori (Fig. 6.17) with its exaggerated, warped and mannered elements and forms. Kari Niskasaari's red brick town hall (1984) in Kiuruvesi, while related to Oulu School work, has mannered postmodern elements, and Ilpo Väisänen and Kyösti Meinilä's Falun red-painted wood Saloila daycare centre (1987) in Oulunsalo features a whimsical silo and vernacular references.

Reinterpreting traditional Finnish architecture, Eric Adlercreutz's Motel Marine (1972) in Tammisaari is sensitively integrated into the historic fabric of the old wooden town. A culturally referenced vernacularism is seen in Kari Järvinen and Timo Airas's small-scale red wooden or brick complexes organized in courtyard groupings with pitched roofs

and clerestories accented with white trim: examples are the wooden Onnimanni daycare centre (1980) in West Säkylä and the red brick school (1985) in Suna, with dynamic sky-lit interior spaces. The white-painted Ylistaro government office complex (1989) uses the same strategies but scales them up to transform the complex into a civic work. Organized around a courtyard the wooden daycare centre (1983) in Lippajärvi by Nurmela, Raimoranta and Tasa is similar in order and expression.

Important adaptive use projects include Aarno Ruusuvuori's refined and elegant Helsinki City Hall remodel and extension (1970–88); Kristian Gullichsen's Pori Art Museum (1981) which repurposes a former customs building; Nurmela, Raimoranta and Tasa's glass addition to the 1884 Fine Arts Academy School (1984) in Helsinki; and Juhani Pallasmaa's Rovaniemi Art Museum (1986), a restrained transformation of a 1930s post bus depot.

Pekka Helin and Tuomo Siitonen created buildings that are well designed and crafted, regardless of form or materials. 'Murikka', the education centre

Fig. 6.18 The forms of Ilmo Valjakka's large, complex and expressive YLE headquarters or broadcast media house (1993) in Helsinki articulate the various functions found within the building. The concept of expressing a building's programme goes back to the Functionalist thinking of the 1920s and 1930s. (Photo: YLE)

of the Finnish Metal Workers' Union (1977), and the UKK Institute (1984) for public health, both in Tampere, and the swimming hall and multi-purpose building (1986) in Hollola are expressive works in concrete, tile and glass. Their red brick, tile and stone UNIC Ltd headquarters (1991) in Helsinki, with its well-composed fenestration, is a more referential and associative work. The Nokia headquarters (1993) in Espoo is a truly sophisticated neo-modern essay in metal and glass. The sod-roofed, wedge-shaped, white concrete Sibelius Quarter residential complex (1993) in Borås, Sweden, references 1930s modernist expression. The white tile and concrete swimming baths (1993) at Forssa incorporate deconstructivist sensibilities, while the Ministry of Social Affairs and Health (1999) in Helsinki has a referential exterior and elegant interior atrium.

In the 1990s, Finnish architects pushed the boundaries of neo-modernism by incorporating constructivist elements and expanding their material palettes. Kaira-Lahdelma-Mahlamäki's Finnish Forest Museum (1994) in Punkaharju incorporates an expressive medley of wood products, as does Lahdelma & Mahlamäki's elementally organized wood-clad Centre for Folk Art (1997) in Kaustinen. Juhani Pallasmaa's SIIDA – the Sámi Museum and the Northern Lapland visitor centre (1998) in Inari – reinterprets a Lapp village, which is the meaning of the word 'siida'. Jan Söderlund and Eero Eske-linen's refined Aspo Group corporate headquarters (1993) in Helsinki has undulating metal and glass curtain walls and sunscreens. Situated along a canal in Rauma is Jokela & Kareoja's refined, white concrete modernist government office building (1992), while their beige brick Hämeenkylä Church (1993) in Vantaa has a luminous interior sanctuary. Esa

The cultural and political connections between the Nordic
countries have an extensive history
and in the post-war period they
have had a common representation
of interests through the Nordic
Council, complemented by the
work of the Nordic Council of
Ministers. After the fall of the
Berlin Wall the German Parliament
resolved to relocate the capital back
to Berlin and an often-considered
idea of a common Nordic embassy
complex was able to be realized
near the Tiergarten (Fig. 6.19).

In 1995 the Austrian-Finnish architectural firm Berger + Parkkinen
won the European Union competition for the project plan and the
one common building open to the
public, the Felleshus or Pan-Nordic
building. The distinguishing feature
of Berger and Parkkinen's design is
the gathering of the five embassy

office buildings within a unifying
sinuous, curving green copper
wall: an architectural landscape
enveloped by a 230-metre-long
and 15-metre-high band of
pre-patinated panels. The space
inside the snaking copper wall is
transected by geometric lanes
or streets which form the entry
plaza and define the edges of the
embassy buildings. Three water
basins between the buildings
metaphorically reference the con-
necting seas between the Nordic
countries.

With the Felleshus forming the
entrance and public space of
the complex (Fig. 6.19, upper
right), the five national embassies
are grouped according to their
geographical relationship. The
integrity of the entire ensemble
and individual expression of each
building results from using a shared

language of materials and elements. The buildings incorporate
wood, metal, glass and stone and
use transparency, louvres, lattices
and perforations to create similarities and contrasts in the individual
expression of each building. While
the buildings are similar yet different, the complex is endowed with
related architectural qualities that
form an experiential and material
ensemble that is both contemporary and respectful of tradition.
The interiors of the embassies are
quite different due to the particular
requirements of each country.

The complex was completed in
1999 and in addition to the work
by Berger + Parkkinen, Sigge/
Viiva Arkkitehtuuri executed the
Finnish Embassy (Figure 6.19,
upper centre), Gert Wingårdh
was responsible for the Swedish
Embassy (Fig. 6.19, upper left),

Laaksonen's pool and leisure complex (1992) in
Siilinjärvi celebrates glazed deconstructivist elements. Kaarina Löfström Architects' Biocentre
(1995) at the University of Helsinki is a sophisticated work in metal and glass, while one of the most
refined of the neo-modern works is the Sanoma
House (1999) by SARC Architects, with its light
steel and double-glazed high-performance envelope
and a full-height public atrium.

Incorporating a variety of influences are several
of the largest buildings in Helsinki executed by Ilmo
Valjakka. The Otavamedia headquarters (1988) has a

tile-clad exterior with constructivist elements while
the impressive YLE headquarters, or broadcast media
house (1993), is dynamic in its elemental expression
(Fig. 6.18). At the same time the large white elementally
organized Finnish National Opera House (1993), by
Eero Hyuvyamyaki, Jukka Karhunen and Risto Parkkinena, was completed on Töölö Bay (see Fig. 6.18).

In 1992 an international competition was held for
a new contemporary art museum in Helsinki. While
the competition was limited to Nordic and Baltic
architects, five international architects were invited
to compete. The winner was a controversial design

Snøhetta designed the Norwegian Embassy (Fig. 6.19, centre left), Palmar Krismundsson undertook the Icelandic Embassy (Fig. 6.19, lower left) and 3XNielsen the Danish Embassy (lower centre). Like the 1930 Stockholm Exhibition, the complex embodies architectural modernity, internationalism and progressiveness, while also being emblematic of a culturally relevant expression of Nordic architecture. It is a fitting architectural conclusion to the twentieth century, while being an excellent springboard to the twenty-first.

Fig. 6.19 The Nordic Embassy complex (1999) in Berlin (by Berger + Parkkinen Architects) is contained within a high green copper wall. The Felleshus or Pan-Nordic building, the one common building open to the public, is shown at upper right. The embassies follow geographically: Finnish (upper centre), Swedish (upper left), Norwegian (centre left), Icelandic (lower left) and Danish (lower centre). (Photo: Courtesy © Günter Schneider, www.guenterschneider.de)

by American architect Steven Holl. Completed in 1998, the museum's name, '*kiasma*', is Finnish for the genetic term 'chiasma' (crosspiece) that was central to Holl's concept for the design.

Heikkinen and Komonen's architecture is a rigorous neo-modernism with constructivist influences, as seen in the Rovaniemi Airport (1992), the McDonald's headquarters (1997) in Helsinki and the European Film College (1993) in Ebeltoft, Denmark. Their Heureka Science Centre (1988) in Vantaa and the extensive Emergency Services College (1992 and 1995) in Kuopio incorporate deconstructivist influences in the organization and formal expression of the buildings.

The emergence of larger and more corporate architectural firms in the North, coupled with the increased amount of work that occurred in the 1990s and the growing global practices of Nordic architects, allowed them to assume more significant roles on the international stage at the end of the twentieth century and positioned them for increased influence in the twenty-first. As the Viking raiders flowed out of the North, beginning in the eighth century to spread their influence from the United Kingdom to Constantinople and over the Mediterranean and even North America, Nordic architects of the current century are bringing progressive designs and practices to the global community.

Globally, architecture has become more of a commodity, with clients, both public and private, seeking cutting-edge designs by 'named' architects to imbue them with the status and recognition achieved through occupying eye-popping and memorable iconic forms and spaces. Internationally a number of architects emerged in the 1990s and early 2000s to form a cavalcade of 'starchitects', and Nordic architects too have entered this panoply of signature practitioners.

Chapter 7

THE GLOBAL AND THE LOCAL: CREATIVE CURRENTS IN NORDIC ARCHITECTURE

THE CREATIVE ARCHITECTURAL OUTPOURings occurring in *fin-de-siècle* Scandinavia were influenced by the desire to express national cultural origins and themes. Nordic architects embraced Functionalism during the late 1920s and early 1930s, though a decade later modified its austerity with traditional materials and forms. During this time modern architecture emerged as the expression for the welfare state. Following the Second World War, Nordic architecture achieved important international recognition for its responsiveness to place, both culturally and materially, and its social vision. Beginning in the 1990s and continuing to the present, Nordic architecture is receiving international attention for its ability to convincingly address and express social, climatic and cultural challenges in today's globalized world.

Today, Nordic architects openly examine a wide variety of architectural ideas and there is a freshness in their approach and a renewed sense of the importance of architecture as a form of cultural expression and creation. A resurgence in Nordic civic and public architecture is resulting in new buildings for cultural, educational and community institutions; buildings produced at an unparalleled level in both quality and quantity. Nordic waterfront developments and, in particular, those in her capitals and larger cities are emblematic of the vitality of these new energies as witnessed by the numerous new concert, opera, museum and commercial venues and housing complexes located on them (*see* Figs 1.12, 6.7, 6.9, 6.11, 7.2, 7.5, 7.12 and 7.15).

For over three quarters of a century Scandinavian architecture has been associated closely to the welfare state. The political, economic and social structures of the Nordic countries have gained global attention for their ability to address complex contemporary challenges. Common to Northern architecture is the humanistic foundation on which the welfare society is based, especially as realized in state-supported buildings for culture, health, education and the young and old. Today, architecture continues to play a robust role demonstrating its ongoing vitality and importance to the welfare state. Twenty-first-century architectural production reveals the vast resources Nordic governments are devoting to enhancing their societies through new housing paradigms, exemplary civic and community buildings and engaging social spaces; all created to reflect the values and ideals of a progressive contemporary society.

While twentieth-century Scandinavian architectural practice was based on the studio model, contemporary practice is increasingly one of diverse, team-based, multidisciplinary approaches. This impacts the scope and scale of public and community projects as well as the size and configuration of practices. Today, firms are often much larger than in the past, some having several hundred employees in addition to operating multiple offices throughout Scandinavia and the world. Like their global counterparts, Nordic architects' engagement in international ideas and trends has been accelerated by the introduction of digital design processes and software, the internet and open-source social interaction. One other impact on global practice is the increase of invited or open architectural competitions for awarding projects or exploring ideas. Taking a page from the Nordic playbook, numerous public and private clients have sought cutting-edge architectural ideas through competitions. One only need visit the web pages of Scandinavian firms to see their remarkable level of participation and success in these competitions. With this in mind and the ready access provided by the internet, this chapter focuses on current works within Scandinavia, as Nordic architects' international activity is another story to be told.

Today, the work of Northern architects graces the cities, campuses and countrysides of Scandinavia as well as the world, making these architects confident about their place internationally. This is all the more important as famous architects from around the globe now build in the North. Often these 'starchitects' produce highly individualized works that embrace a well-recognized aesthetic that is repeated globally; works that are often created with scant respect for locale or the challenges of the North. With a number of Northern architects joining the ranks of 'starchitects' the issue reverses; in international practice are Scandinavian architects transforming their ideas in ways responsive to non-Nordic conditions? Or are they, too, creating highly individualized, aestheticized works that could be located anywhere? Again, it is a story yet to be written.

In this climate of commodification there is concern that the cultural and material specificity long associated with Scandinavian architecture is disappearing into a more global universality. Is the North losing its reliance on place and tradition? As Nordic architects continue grappling with brick, pine, granite, concrete, glass, metals and planting as the basis for contemporary building, three threads emerge. First, in keeping with international directions, is the creation of architecture primarily focused on expressive, explorative and progressive formal and spatial results. Second is the continued refinement and development of neo-modernism now transformed by advancements in metals and glass, especially new glazing applications and opportunities. Last is the continued confidence to create buildings in which site, culture and local conditions are acknowledged or reinterpreted in a distinctive place-based manner.

But it is the interaction between these threads that forms the creative currents engaging the global and the local. Many practices span the three, through weaving the pluralistic world of international ideas with the long-standing foundation of Nordic tradition and restraint.

Denmark

Scandinavian housing developments during the 1990s pointed to a new expressiveness, but little prepared the North for the housing propositions put forth by PLOT, Bjarke Ingels Group (BIG) and JDS Architects, among others in Denmark. PLOT's VM Housing (2005) (Fig. 7.1), in the Ørestad district of Copenhagen, with its sloped glass façade and spikey meshed balconies, was the first in a sequence of avant-garde housing projects. PLOT dissolved into two firms: the Bjarke Ingels Group (BIG) and JDS Architects. BIG produced two extraordinary works in Ørestad: the stepped-form Mountain Dwellings (2008) incorporated wood cladding and planting, while, formed around a courtyard, 8 House (2010) incorporates metal panels and a sloped sodded roof. JDS Architects' TAD/Iceberg complex (2013) on the Aarhus docks recalls iceberg shapes by using abstract sloping with pointy white concrete forms and blue glass balconies.

Other progressive housing projects include Henning Larsen Architects' undulating metal and glass 'The Wave' (2009) in Vejle; Lundgaard & Tranberg's round metal, wood and glass Tietgen Student Hall (2006) in Ørestad and their sloped-form white modernist Havneholmen housing estate (2009) in Copenhagen. AART Architects' metal-panelled Bikuben student residence (2006) in Ørestad is formed around a double spiral atrium, while JJW Arkitekter's 'Seed Silo' (2005, with Dutch firm MVRDV) incorporates two concrete seed silos on Copenhagen's waterfront.

Important civic projects bear witness to the Danish investment in major cultural venues, many

Fig. 7.1 First in a sequence of avant-garde housing projects, PLOT's VM Housing (2005) in the Ørestad district of Copenhagen provided a new paradigm of expression for housing, with its sloped glass façade and spikey meshed balconies. (Photo: Krysta Mae Dimick)

being located on existing waterways, reclaimed docks or former ship yards. Henning Larsen's stately and refined limestone and glass Copenhagen Opera House (2005) and Lundgaard & Tranberg's Royal Danish Playhouse (2008), with its sophisticated copper and glass detailing, beckon across the Copenhagen harbour to each other in an evocative architectural dance (Fig. 7.2). There is also 3XN's extraordinary powerful and sculptural metal-clad Blue Planet Aquarium (2013) in Copenhagen. Outside the capital is Schmidt Hammer Lassen's cubic red brick 'ARoS' or Aarhus Art Museum (2003) with its sensuous curving multi-storey interior and artist Òlafur Eliasson's circular skywalk entitled 'your rainbow panorama' (2011). Jørn Utzon's last work, the metal tent-like roofed Utzon Centre (2008) on Aalborg's harbour, has an impressively lit interior. In 2003 Utzon became the second Scandinavian architect to receive the prestigious Pritzker Prize.

Another form of urban intervention is occurring; new public promenades along harbours and waterfronts for recreation and leisure. Exemplary projects in Copenhagen include PLOT's undulating wood-finished Maritime Youth House (2004) – a youth centre and sailing club – and their recreational harbour baths (2002) on Island Brygge. The Kalvebod Waves (2008), by JDS Architects + Urban-Agency, is a wood and concrete structure weaving and undulating along the waterfront (Fig. 7.3). The sinuous bridge *Cykelslangen* or 'Bicycle Snake' (2014), by Dissing + Weitling, ensures fast and unhindered bike passage between several of the city's islands. Elsewhere, JDS Architects + Urban Agency's harbour bath (2014) in Fåborg provides numerous ways to approach and engage the water. These works represent progressive investments in unique public amenities.

BIG and JDS Architects also pushed the architectural envelope in other projects. BIG's Superkilen

Fig. 7.2 Henning Larsen's Copenhagen Opera House (2005) and Lundgaard & Tranberg's Royal Danish Playhouse (2008) respond to each other across the Copenhagen harbour. (Photo: By Markus Bernet (Own work) [CC BY-SA 2.5 (http://creativecommons.org/licenses/by-sa/2.5)], via Wikimedia Commons)

Fig. 7.3 The Kalvebod Waves (2008), by JDS Architects + Urban-Agency, creates a waterfront stage for the expected and unexpected to occur. (Photo: Krysta Mae Dimick)

(2012, with Topotek1) is an evocative public park in Copenhagen that has three distinct qualitative, metaphoric zones – a red square, a black market and a green park; while their unique boat-shaped sunken concrete and glass National Maritime Museum (2013) is located between Kronborg Castle and the new Culture Yard in Helsingør. JDS Architects executed the elegant steel structure world championship ski-jump (2011) in Holmenkollen outside Oslo.

Larger Danish firms have created works that weave together the threads of contemporary Nordic developments. Henning Larsen Architects' more expressive work includes the spatially dynamic Viborg Town Hall (2011), a glass superstructure surmounting a stone and sod-roofed base, while their earth-integrated Moesgård Museum (2013) outside Aarhus is a concrete wedge seeming to pivot out of the site. The powerful triangular learning centre (2014) at Campus Kolding of the University of Southern Denmark incorporates an active façade system of 1,600 perforated triangular steel shutters to manipulate natural light. Neo-modern projects include the IT University of Copenhagen (2004) with its striking central space, the black metal and glass curved-form Winghouse office building (2010) in Ørestad and the concrete and aluminium sports complex (2014) at Ystad with its computerized LED light programme that activates the façade.

Schmidt Hammer Lassen's 'Crystal' (2011) in the Vesterbro district for Nykredit is an elegant metal and glass sloped and faceted prism, while their formally fragmented Dokk1 Urban Mediaspace (2015) on the Aarhus harbour is the largest public library in Scandinavia. The Nykredit headquarters (2001) in Copenhagen, with its large interior atrium, and the glass and concrete curved free-form Halmstad Library (2006) in Sweden which projects over the Nissan River represent their neo-modern projects.

3XN explores evocative forms, as exemplified in the diagonally striped green glass façades of the Saxo Bank (2008) in Hellerup; the uniquely shaped Middelfart savings bank (2010) with its dramatic roof-scape of 83 prism-like skylights; their AC Hotel Bella Sky (2011) (Fig. 7.4) in Ørestad which has two curved

Fig. 7.4 3XN has created powerful and stunning works in the North, as is witnessed by the two inclined and faceted towers of the AC Hotel Bella Sky (2011) in Ørestad. (Photo: Krysta Mae Dimick)

inclined faceted towers; and the granite folded-form 'Plassen' cultural centre (2012) in Molde, Norway, which incorporates two amphitheatres for outdoor jazz performances. Neo-modern works include the FIH Erhvervsbank (2002) in Copenhagen with its sliding aluminium sunscreens; the Ørestad College (2007), formed around a community atrium with coloured semi-transparent operable glass louvres modulating the façade; and the refined travertine- and glass-faceted Horten headquarters (2009) in Copenhagen.

Lundgaard & Tranberg's four-storey glass 'Wedge' (2006), with its storey-height exterior moveable screens of wood, matte glass and copper, is part of their Copenhagen Business School (2007) and near the Kalvebod wharf in Copenhagen is their curved undulating green glass SEB bank headquarters (2010). They reinterpreted traditional pitched-roof forms in the Sorø Art Museum addition (2011) while incorporating custom-made ceramic shingles, and created the sustainable forward-looking red brick office building (2014) in Langelinie.

A number of Danish firms have created powerful, stunning works. AART Architects' multi-use Culture Yard (2010) in Helsingør near Kronborg Castle and the National Maritime Museum is a vibrant faceted steel, aluminium and glass structure adapted over traditional brick harbour buildings. Their Inspiria Science Centre (2010) in Grålum, Norway, is a dynamic sloped wrap-around metal and glass form, while the Adult Education Centre (2013, with ZENI Architects) for VUC Syd on the Haderslev waterfront has an elegant light-filled white atrium space and dynamic rotated floor plates.

Dorte Mandrup Architects' work includes the elevated glass cube treetop-like grotto addition (2001) to the renovated Holmbladsgade neighbourhood centre in Copenhagen; the cubic aluminium mesh and panelled Herstedlund community centre (2009) in Albertslund; the playful Ama'r children's culture house (2012) in Copenhagen, with its aluminium-clad evocatively shaped form; and the sharp white steel sailing tower (2015) on the Aarhus harbour. JJW

Arkitekter's green concrete senior citizens' housing (2012) in Ørestad has playfully extruded balconies on the façade, while their Sydhavn School (2014), in Copenhagen, uses a large evocative stair-like form to organize the complex. NORD Architects executed the cylindrical glass and metal Natural Science Centre (2011) in Bjerringbro and the expressive pointy-roofed wood and aluminium Copenhagen Centre for Cancer and Health (2012).

Since the last quarter of the twentieth century, neo-modernism has been a staple in the canon of Danish architecture. PLH Arkitekter's gentling bowing triangular Aller Media headquarters (2009) in Copenhagen is a refined essay in metal and glass. In the context of its red brick surroundings TRANSFORM Architects' Confederation of Danish Industries headquarters (2013) in Copenhagen has a monumental neon screen covering its glass and metal façade. Arkitema Architects' swimming stadium at Bellahøj (2009) in Copenhagen is a Miesian-influenced white structurally expressive steel and glass pavilion, while KHR Arkitekter's eight-storey brick and glass Ørestad School and Library (2012) is a subtle refined work.

Danish architects have also created buildings where site, culture and local conditions are acknowledged or reinterpreted. The red façade of the Vibeeng School (2014) in Haslev, by Arkitema Architects, incorporates playful and colourful forms and spaces, while PLH Arkitekter executed the refined solid brick National Archives (2009) with its rune-like façade reliefs that extend into the landscape design. Keeping with tradition, several religious works have stunning white interiors allowing for a wondrous play of light: Friis & Moltke's white Functionalist-inspired hospital chapel (2000) in Aalborg and two churches by Regnbuen Arkitekter. The Antovorskov Church (2005) in Slagelse and the Dybkær Church (2010) in Silkeborg have traditional brick exteriors, courtyards and well-crafted interior spaces, allowing subtle plays of light and shadow.

Sustainability informs Christensen & Co. Architects Green Lighthouse (2009) for the University of Copenhagen, the first carbon-neutral building in Denmark; their education building (2013) at the Technical University of Denmark Lyngby campus; and the expansive education centre Navitas (2014) on the Aarhus waterfront, Denmark's largest low-energy building. GPP Arkitekter's circular South Energy headquarters (2013), in Esbjerg, has a spacious atrium while utilizing low and alternative energy sources, while Arkitema Architects produced an essay on sustainability and energy efficiency in the dark steel and glass House of Vestas (2011), headquarters of Vestas Wind Systems in Aarhus.

Sweden

In Stockholm, White Arkitekter is responsible for the highly visible Water Front development (2011) which includes the congress and concert hall with its free-form billowing metal veils, an office block and hotel (Fig. 7.5) and the perforated metal multi-purpose Tele2 arena (2013) that resembles a wicker basket

which then becomes a colourful lantern at night. Johan Celsing Arkitektkontor executed the refined metal and glass flatiron-shaped Bonniers Konsthall (2006). Outside Stockholm, Wingårdh Arkitektur's glazed universeum (2001), or science centre, in Gothenburg engages its site through an open structure, while the large multi-purpose Malmö arena (2008) is a refined essay in metal and glass. Tham & Videgård produced the large red perforated steel Modern Museum (2009) in Malmö and the Kalmar Museum of Art (2008), a cube of black wooden panels and large glazed openings. Three Danish firms created major civic works in Sweden: Henning Larsen's modulated reflective glass and metal panelled Uppsala Concert and Congress Hall (2007) or 'Uppsala Crystal' (Fig. 7.6); Schmidt Hammer Lassen's large multi-building 'Malmö Live' Concert Hall and Conference Centre (2015); and Christensen & Co. Architects' green glass and steel Lund City Hall (2014) with its well-detailed atrium.

Sweden, too, has larger firms creating works weaving the threads of contemporary Nordic

Fig. 7.5 In Stockholm, White Arkitekter's highly visible Water Front complex (2011), with its free-form billowing metal veils animating the congress and concert hall, is framed by the gridded office block and hotel behind. (Photo: By Holger.Ellgaard (Own work) [CC BY-SA 3.0 (http://creativecommons.org/licenses/by-sa/3.0)], via Wikimedia Commons)

Fig. 7.6 Danish architect Henning Larsen's Uppsala concert and congress hall (2007) is a split cubic form with a sculptural reflective metallic and glass façade and is referred to locally as the 'Crystal'. (Photo: Krysta Mae Dimick)

developments. White Arkitekter is responsible for the dynamic wooden circular Kastrup Sea Bath (2005) in Tårnby (Denmark) and the sculptural Hasle Harbour Bath (2013) on the island of Bornholm. In addition to their numerous civic, commercial and housing projects, the firm won a number of Swedish Environmental Protection Agency competitions for visitor centres in national parks and nature reserves: the large wood-clad Vattenriket visitor centre (2010) in the wetlands near Kristianstad incorporates walking causeways and an amphitheatre; the Falun red-painted Naturum visitor centre (2013) in Ekenäs is a small-scale complex referencing coastal fishing villages; and the vertical wood and glass-clad Naturum Vänerskärgården, Victoriahuset (2013), is located near Lake Vänern. In collaboration with Henning Larsen, they created the engaging vertical wood and glass complex for the art campus at the University of Umeå (2008–12); with its School of Architecture, School of Design and vertically expressive Art Museum.

Wingårdh Arkitektur has executed a series of exceptional works, many neo-modern in realization. The tessellated 34-storey façade of the Victoria Tower (2011) in Kista is cloaked in triangular-paned glass while the Ericsson headquarters (2010) has a spectacular irregular gouge in its curtain-wall façade. The Spira theatre complex (2011) in Jönköping is sheathed in vertical coloured glazing and metal panels and the circular mixed-use Kuggen or Chalmers education building (2011) in Gothenburg has a vibrant multi-coloured glass and metal curtain wall. Their refined triangular Gina Tricot headquarters (2010) in Borås uses white screen-printed glazing, while the sloped triangular form Aula Medica (2011) for the Karolinska Institute in Solna uses six types of glass in an abstract pattern (Fig. 7.7).

Sweden, too, has had its inventive, cutting-edge projects. Two works in Stockholm by Tham & Videgård demonstrate their inventiveness: the undulating amoeba-like Tellus Nursery School (2010) with its yellow-painted wood-ribbed exterior with punched windows, and the oval red steel and glass KTH School of Architecture (2015) is surmounted by a large light

Fig. 7.7 Wingårdh Arkitektur's sloped and curved Aula Medica (2011) for the Karolinska Institute in Solna uses six types of glass in an abstract pattern composed of triangular pieces. (Photo: By Holger.Ellgaard (Own work) [CC BY-SA 3.0 (http://creativecommons.org/licenses/by-sa/3.0)], via Wikimedia Commons)

monitor. In Malmö, Krook & Tjäder's P-Hus Dockan (2009) parking garage has a plant-covered CorTen steel and glass façade, while artist and designer Monika Gora's Glass Bubble (2007) in Malmö's Västra Hamnen neighbourhood is both a sculpture and greenhouse.

In central Lund the new cathedral forum and visitors' centre (2011), by Carmen Izquierdo, engages the historic Arken house yet powerfully expresses its new functions both formally and spatially. The exterior is clad in a bronze-coloured brass alloy skin while the interior is exposed concrete. Jais Arkitekter's appealing red-panelled fifteen-storey Bohus 5 tower (2014) in Malmö is articulated with extruded bay windows.

Neo-modernism also has additional adherents in Sweden. Magnus Ståhl Arkitekter's elegant asymmetrical stainless-steel Bridge Apaté (2001) spans the Sickla Canal in Stockholm, while Reflex Arkitekter executed the Vasagatan 7 office complex (2009) with its intricate façade of glass boxes and extruded metal elements. In Malmö, Metro Arkitekter executed the large steel and glass sloped shed form central station (2011) and the Erika car park (2010), with its façade of white glass boxes that creates an engaging urban nightscape. Krook & Tjäder's elegant riverside triangular SVT/SR building (2008) in Gothenburg is a light structural essay in glass and metal.

In keeping with Nordic traditions, Johan Celsing Arkitektkontor's red-brown brick and concrete Arsta Church (2008) in Stockholm recalls earlier brutalist-inspired works, while his stone-clad

Near the Arctic Circle the village of Harads, north of Luleå in Swedish Lapland, is a unique place to engage nature and architecture. With distinctive and idiosyncratic designed rooms literally placed in the trees, the Treehotel provides guests with a place where nature, sustainable values, comfort and contemporary design combine. Inspired by Jonas Selberg Augustsén's movie 'The Tree Lover' (2008), a philosophic story about the importance of trees to humans, the hotel offers guests the opportunity to enjoy nature among the trees while simultaneously providing distinctive architectural experiences.

The rooms are suspended 4–6 metres above the ground within the trees to provide spectacular views of the Lule River and its valley and of kilometres of forests. Material and construction techniques have minimized environmental impact as the rooms have been built among live trees without destroying them. Each treeroom, while incorporating ecological and sustainable values, is a unique creation by a leading Scandinavian architect. The designs combine with the quiet of the forest to create feelings of excitement, relaxation and contemplation.

The idiosyncratic nature of each treeroom is articulated in its name and architectural form. The Mirrorcube (2010) by Tham & Videgård is a cubic aluminium frame sheathed with reflective glass, creatively melding building with forest (Fig. 7.8). The Cabin (2010) by Cyrén & Cyrén is like a capsule or foreign body in the tree. The branch-covered Bird's Nest (2010), by Bertil Harström of Inrednings Gruppen, is a metaphorical nest on the exterior protecting a contemporary interior. The Falun red-painted ironically named pyramidal Blue Cone (2010) by Sandellsandberg has a laminated birch interior. The UFO (2010), literally a saucer-shaped capsule of durable composite material, is also by Bertil Harström. The cross-shaped Dragon Fly (2013) by Rintala Eggertsson Architects has a CorTen steel exterior and wood interior. Simple wood detailing characterizes the exterior of Bertil Harström's round two-storey wood Tree Sauna (2010) as compared to its refined interior finishes.

metaphoric 'Stone in the Forest' crematorium (2013) with its white interiors is a very worthy recent addition to the architecture of the famous Woodland Cemetery. In Ödeshög Wingårdh Arkitektur created the U-formed thatched-roof Tåkern visitor centre (2012), inspired by local vernacular style.

Finland

A significant urban development in downtown Helsinki is the strategically located Kamppi Centre (2006) on the site of the old bus station behind the 1930s Functionalist Glass Palace (Fig. 7.9). This impressive multi-use facility houses a major transportation hub in addition to commercial, offices and residential units by a consortium of architectural offices, including those of Juhani Pallasmaa (who led the design team) and his collaborators: Helin&Co Architects, Marja-Riitta Norri Architects and ARX Architects. While the buildings are executed in a refined and expressive constructivism, the complex also includes K2S Architects' elegantly crafted curved wooden Kamppi Chapel of Silence (2012) (Fig. 7.10). A block away is Helin&Co Architects' triangular annexe to the Finnish Parliament House

In Norway, two examples of visitors' lodgings having a strongly developed relationship with the landscape include Jensen & Skodvin Arkitektkontor's Juvet Landscape Hotel (2008) in Valldal; this is a minimalist intervention of nine detached rooms in wood and glass engaging its striking river-edge site. The glass walls of the austere units erase the boundaries between inside and out. Famed Norwegian polar explorer Børge Ousland selected architect Snorre Stinessen to design the four sea cabins (2015) for his resort on Manshausen Island, an abandoned fishing outpost above the Arctic Circle. The four cabins, three of them cantilevered over the water on the harbour's old stone jetty, feature glass on three sides for 270-degree views of the island.

Fig. 7.8 In Swedish Lapland, the Treehotel's six architecturally unique rooms are suspended from the trees. The Mirrorcube (2010) by Tham & Videgård creatively melds building with trees while providing a wonderful view of the Lule River valley. (Photo: Courtesy Treehotel, © Peter Lundstrom, WDO)

(2004), with its elegant glass atrium and contextually responsive exterior form (*see* Fig. 7.9, centre right). Across Mannerheiminaukio, in a reclaimed train yard between Aalto's Finlandia Hall and Stephen Holl's Kiasma, is LPR Architects' Helsinki Music Centre (2011) with its green copper-panelled auditorium volume set within an elegant glazed foyer. Under construction east of the Music Centre is ALA Architects' new Helsinki Central Library, scheduled to be completed in 2018.

Recent Finnish civic works include Helin&Co Architects' neo-modern Sello chamber music auditorium and Juvenalia School of Music, with the regional library (2003), in Espoo, forming an impressive cultural complex. The Sibelius Hall (2000) in Lahti, by Kimmo Lintula and Hannu Tikka, is a box within a box; a rationalist steel and glass exterior protects the wooden concert hall enclosure. The complex also includes the Forest Hall, with wood columns and framing referencing tree branches. Lahdelma & Mahlamäki Architects' dramatic Maritime Centre Vellamo (2008) on the Kotka waterfront is a large curving and faceted wedge-shaped form in metal and glass. ARK-House Architects' modest but studied Seafarers' Centre (2009) in Helsinki creates sinuous spaces using simple curved wood and glass walls.

Fig. 7.9 A significant new urban complex in the centre of Helsinki is the strategically located Kamppi Centre (2006) and Narinkkatori Square. As is often the case, forest, rock and water are present in Helsinki's urban context. (Photo: Courtesy City of Helsinki, photographer Suomen Ilmakuva Oy)

Anttinen Oiva Architects' Helsinki University main library (2010) has red brick façades with gridded windows, large curved glass areas and a multi-storey oval white atrium. The Korundi House of Culture (2011) by Juhani Pallasmaa expands the Rovaniemi Art Museum complex by adding a refined and elegant concert hall.

Neo-modern sensibilities abound in current Finnish architecture: Helin&Co Architects' Sitra Price Waterhouse Coopers complex (2000) in Helsinki is a refined essay in CorTen steel and glass. Their Finnforest Modular Office (2005) in Tapiola is a symphony in wood and modular prefabricated building components. SARC Architects designed the all-glazed Sonera building (2000) in Helsinki, with its colourful glass screening, and the double-glazed Kone building (2001) in Espoo near the Nokia headquarters. Their

rationalist Miesian-inspired METLA Forest Research Centre (2004) in Joensuu is one of Finland's largest complexes executed in wood.

Heikkinen and Komonen invigorate neo-modernism with constructivist and deconstructivist forms, as seen in their Rovaniemi Airport extension (2000); the Vuotalo centre (2000) in the Vuosaari suburb of Helsinki; the large Mediacentre Lume (2000) complex at the Aalto University School of Art and Design in Helsinki; and the Hämeenlinna Regional Archive (2010) with its image-etched concrete façade. Their Flooranaukio housing complex (2012) in Helsinki combines dual images; a rational brick exterior with a more undulating painterly interior courtyard.

Lahdelma & Mahlamäki Architects executed the glass and steel Vaasa Library (2001) built around the

Fig. 7.10 In the Kamppi Centre is K2S Architects' elegantly crafted curved wooden Kamppi Chapel of Silence (2012), a place of quiet, repose and contemplation in a busy downtown world. Here one is reminded of Reima Pietilä's idea of 'caves of wood' being the dream of forest people. (Photo: Krysta Mae Dimick)

JKMM's shingle-clad Viikki Church (2005) has an elegant articulated wood ceiling and interior, while their refined Turku Main Library (2006), with its abstract modernist elemental expression, is superbly detailed. Conical skylights punctuate the sloping concrete form of the children's house (2011) on Saunalahti Gulf in Espoo, with its sculptural play yard. The elegant, abstract and austere city library (2012) for Seinäjoki is a three-volume copper-clad structure successfully interacting with Alvar Aalto's earlier civic centre complex (Fig. 7.11). The campus-like city-block-scaled OP Financial Group headquarters (2015) in Helsinki has a creative, expressive fenestration pattern.

Colour informs ARK-House Architects' work, which includes the circular glass and metal Korona Information Centre (2000) at the University of Helsinki Viikki Campus and the AV in School (2001) building at the Aalto University School of Art and Design with its façade of semaphore-coloured corrugated metal panels. Auer & Sandås Architects executed two wonderfully colourful and playful daycare centres: the Tuomarila daycare centre (2008) and the elementally expressed Suurpelto children's house (2014), both in Espoo.

Arto Sipinen's triangular Innova office tower (2004) in Jyväskylä is sophisticatedly expressed in white steel and glass, while Käpy and Simo Paavilainen's local government pensions' institution office building (2004) in Helsinki is an essay in white metal and glass, with an elegant sky-lit atrium. The floating Arctia headquarters (2013) in Katajanokka, by K2S Architects, has refined black perforated steel façades recalling icebreaker hulls, and elegant lacquered wood interiors. Huttu-Hiltunen's CCC Group headquarters (2000) in Oulunsalo is an elemental constructivist composition in CorTen steel, white screening and glass. Kai Wartiainen's Ruoholahti High Tech Centre (2001) is a crane-like structure on the west harbour in Helsinki housing IT companies and education facilities (Fig. 7.12).

Arresting religious works include Juha Leiviskä's striking white planar interiors in the red and white

old municipal archive, the Miesian-inspired glass and concrete Rauma Library (2003) and the red brick Aaltoesque Main Library (2005) in Lohja with cone-shaped light monitors. Their Kastelli School and Community Centre (2014) in Oulu, a folded metal form covering four square pavilions, is accented with colourful metal panels and the wood-clad Finnish nature centre 'Haltia' (2013) in Espoo is a form within a form.

Fig. 7.11 The elegant and abstract new city library in Seinäjoki (2012) by JKMM Architects creates a dialogue with the original library by Alvar Aalto (1965). While respecting the architecturally and culturally significant Seinäjoki town centre complex, JKMM created three engaging copper-clad volumes that make a bold contemporary architectural statement. The tower of Aalto's 'Cross of the Plains Church' (1960) is visible in the background. (Photo: Courtesy JKMM Architects, © Mika Huisman, photographer)

Fig. 7.12 Kai Wartiainen's Ruoholahti High Tech centre (2001) is a series of crane-like structures on the west harbour in Helsinki, housing both IT companies and education facilities. (Photo: Krysta Mae Dimick)

Fig. 7.13 Designated as the city's cultural centre, the Bjørvika neighbourhood in central Oslo has been transformed from a container port on the Oslofjord by new civic buildings and commercial developments. Across the water from the Oslo Opera House (see Fig. 1.12) is the Barcode Project, a row of new multi-purpose high-rise buildings. (Photo: Krysta Mae Dimick)

brick Church of the Good Shepherd (2002) in the Helsinki suburb of Pakila; Matti Sanaksenaho's copper-sheathed boat-shaped St Henry's Ecumenical Art Chapel (2005) in Turku, with its warm interior structure of glued laminated timber; and Järvinen & Nieminen's patinated copper Laajasalo Church (2003) in Helsinki, with its refined wooden interior spaces. Lassila Hirvilammi Architects produced three significant churches: the copper-clad church and parish centre (2004) in Klaukkala, with curved wooden ceiling and free-standing copper and glass bell tower; the cubic handcut log structure of Kärsämäki Church (2004) with its pyramidal roof and shingle cladding; and the Koukkala Church (2010) in Jyväskylä with its wood lattice sanctuary and referential slate form and bell tower.

Organized around a glass atrium, Sigge Architects/Viiva Arkkitehtuuri's town hall (2012) in Kirkkonummi is a cubic volume in brick and glass with randomly placed perforated copper panels. Their circular TYS Ikituuri student housing tower (2011) in Turku has a colour-aged copper-tiled skin and glazed balconies, while the Pyynikki social and health-care centre (2013) in Tampere is a multi-winged copper and glass complex.

HALO Architects' Sami cultural centre and parliament house Sajos (2012) in Inari has elliptical parliament and auditorium spaces placed within a curved cross-shaped form. The rough wooden-slatted exterior creates a monolithic presence contrasting with the finely finished wood interior.

Norway

The Bjørvika neighbourhood in central Oslo has been transformed from a container port on the Oslofjord by new commercial and civic developments. Evolving as the city's new cultural centre, the area contains Snøhetta's iconic Oslo Opera House (2008) (see Fig. 1.12) with its sloping granite and marble plaza engaging the water and providing panoramic views of the city. Across the way is the Barcode Project (Fig. 7.13), a row of multi-purpose high-rise buildings, metaphorically recalling the bar and space pattern of the ubiquitous bar code. Beginning the sequence is A-Lab's metal and glass Price Water-house Coopers headquarters (2008), followed by Solheim & Jacobsen's KLP building (2010) with its two entwined towers – one in white stone with punched window openings, the other in glass and metal. The abstract glass and white metal curtain wall of Snøhetta's Deloitte building or 'The Glacier' (2012) was inspired by a calving glacier. Dark Arkitekter's Visma building (2011) has a metal and glass pixel-lated façade making the scale of the building difficult to read. Last is the DnB NOR headquarters (2012) by MVRDV, Dark Arkitekter and A-Lab, consisting of three buildings with different expressive qualities. Much more is planned for the area, especially public and civic works: the new Oslo central station by Space Group is currently being completed, while the Munch/Stenersen Museum and Deichman Library will soon begin construction.

Important Norwegian civic projects include Jarmund/Vigsnæs Arkitekter's large evocative folded copper-clad Svalbard science centre (2004) in Longyearbyen with its wood interiors, and the waterfront-sited Stavanger Concert Hall (2012), with is faceted glass lobby, dynamic hanging sculptures and brick theatre volume, by RATIO Arkitekter. A-Lab's refined prefabricated steel and concrete Arctic cul-tural centre (2008) in Hammerfest, the world's north-ernmost city, is sheathed in an etched glass skin. Sverre Fehn's National Museum – Architecture (2008) is an elegant glass and concrete addition to Christian Grosch's 1830 neoclassical bank building in Oslo. Helen and Hard's wood-ribbed library and cultural centre (2011) in Vennesla is a sensuous combination of wood and natural light.

The elementally expressed cultural centre (2015) in Stjørda and wood-sheathed Romsdal Folk Museum (2015) in Molde, with its animated pointed roof forms, are by Reiulf Ramstad Architects. Niels Torp Architects' cultural centre (2009) in Larvik has an undulating roof over an elegant glass pavilion. The Finnish firm ALA Architects' Kilden Performing Arts Centre (2012) in Kristiansand is a strong conceptual work, refined in its execution. Its wedge-shaped black metal exterior contains a powerful cantilevered undu-lating wooden lobby ceiling.

Snøhetta has created a number of exemplary works: the elementally organized Hamar Town Hall (2000) is executed in several materials including a CorTen steel and glass bell tower, while the wedge-shaped Bærum cultural centre (2003) in Sandvika is a glass-sheathed prism. Boldly inserting itself through its hilly site is the curved-roofed Petter Dass Museum (2007) in Alstahaug. The Clarion Hotel Energy (2014) in Stavanger is a tilted lamella volume of reflective metal and glass, while the Väven cultural centre (2014, with White Arkitekter) in Umeå, Sweden, is a sophis-ticated weaving of glass and white panelling.

A-Lab's Statoil headquarters (2012) on the Fornebu waterfront near Oslo is a most evocative work, with its five metal lamella forms stacked on each other in a seemingly random manner (Fig. 7.14); its fenes-tration recalls computer punch cards. Lund+Slaatto Architects' roadside restaurant Marché (2009) in Lier Nord is a green copper-clad folded form with wooden interior; their Oslo Z (2010) is an evocative commercial structure; and the headquarters for NSB and Gjensidige (2013) in Oslo is a cubic stone and glass volume with an elegantly detailed atrium. Lund Hagem Architects' Institute for Informatics (2010) at the Blindern campus of the University of Oslo seems a cousin of the NSB headquarters, its long black steel upper portion hovering over the glass and brick ground floor.

Kristin Jarmund Architects' concrete Wessterdals School of Communication (2011) in Oslo is a black shed form with an engaging window arrangement and colourful yellow interiors, while their second-ary school (2009) in Gjerdrum is a multi-material, expressively playful elemental composition. The firm's modernist-inspired Nydalen subway station (2003) in Oslo has a neon and sound 'Tunnel of Light' experi-ence, while the Fokus Bank (2005) in Oslo is an essay in black stone, glass and wood. Their white 'Treasury' or Department of Tax and Revenue building (2007) in Sandvika achieves a modernist expression through its wrap-around glazing.

The elementally organized and pointed roof forms of Reiulf Ramstad Architects' civic work are repeated in the wood-sheathed folded-form Fagerborg Kindergarten (2010) in Oslo, while the community church (2014) in Knarvik, with its powerful bell tower, is a folded wooden volume abstractly interpreting traditional medieval church forms. More neo-modern is the Østfold University College (2006), with its fully glazed multi-storey lower level surmounted by a cantilevered metal and glass top floor.

As with her Nordic cousins, neo-modernism is also important in Norway. Narud Stokke Wiig's light-filled Bjørnholt Secondary School (2007) in Oslo achieves an elegant industrial imagery. Formally and spatially impressive, Niels Torp's BI Campus (2005) in Nydalen, Oslo's independent business school, is like a small city with the entire college environment in one building. The Bergen fish market (2015) by Eder Biesel Arkitekter, an elevated glass box with expressed vertical coloured wood panels, creates

a rhythmic presence on the waterfront (Fig. 7.15), while the glazed ground floor intensifies the building's floating quality. The vertical wedge-form Rica Seilet Hotel (2002) in Molde by Kjell Kosberg is an elegant glass and metal tower on the city's waterfront.

A number of Norwegian works continue to be rooted in locale and tradition: Kari Nissen Brodtkorb continues her refined brick and black-painted steel expression in the Lysaker Bygge mixed-use complex (2004) in Bærum; the House 25 mixed-use complex (2007) on the Tjurholmen dock in Oslo; and the Region House 'Dockums' office complex (2011) in Malmö: all are organized around courtyard spaces or atriums. SPINN Arkitekter, Various Architects and the Danish firm CEBRA executed the large wood-sheathed Mesterfjellet School (2014) with its rhythmic window patterns and colourful atrium. Three triangular light scoops surmount the refined wood and glass form of Askim Lanttro Arkitekter's Bok og

Fig. 7.14 A-Lab's Statoil regional and international office (2012), at Fornebu outside Oslo, is an evocative work with five plate-like lamella forms stacked on each other in a seemingly random manner. (Photo: Hans A. Rosbach (Own work) [CC-BY-SA 3.0 (http://creativecommons.org/licenses/by-sa/3.0)], via Wikimedia Commons)

Fig. 7.15 The Bergen fish market (2015) by Eder Biesel Arkitekter is an elevated glass box with brightly coloured vertical wood panels; it creates a rhythmic presence on the waterfront, exemplifying contemporary Nordic neo-modernism. (Photo: Krysta Mae Dimick)

Appreciating Nature's All-Mightiness: Architecture along Norway's National Tourist Routes

Norway's scenic tourist routes are unique, as eighteen routes weave 1,850km over the country's rugged and picturesque landscape. The National Tourist Routes initiative, begun in 1994 and originated by the Norwegian Public Roads Administration, has resulted in a number of shelters, scenic lookouts, hiking trails, rest areas and bird-watching pavilions built along the winding backcountry roads; routes with untarnished and powerful scenery. By emphasizing small-scale, landscape and place-driven designs that also achieve a high level of innovation, the works are sensitive as well as stunning as they enrich, frame and accent their sites. These evocative designs are as much a draw as the scenery; nature bonds with architecture.

Currently about 130 structures have been finished, with full completion of about 250 structures planned for 2023. Initially the architecture firms involved have been from Norway, with many now-well-known firms being unknown at the time of their selection. Recognizing young, emerging architects is an important part of the procurement process. Only recently have international names been added; Swiss architect Peter Zumthor and the late French-American artist Louise Bourgeois collaborated on the evocative Steilneset Memorial (2011) in Vardø. Zumthor, a Pritzker Architecture Prize winner, is completing 'Allmannajuvet', that tells the story of the zinc mines in Sauda.

The range, scale and size of the projects vary greatly. 3RW Arkitektur and Smedsvig Landskap's Ørnesvingen Viewpoint (2005) overlooking the Geirangerfjord is spectacular, while the costal Askvågen viewpoint (2006) near Møre og Romsdal is more minimalist, and their slate and yellow composite material restrooms at Hereiane (2007) in Hardanger juxtapose traditional forms with contemporary interiors. Aurora Landskap created a wooden walkway with observation platforms (2007) for viewing the dramatic Devil's Teeth cliffs on Senja Island. Pushak Architects' Snefjord rest stop (2005) features copper-sheathed 'bench boxes' protecting people from the wind. For viewing the Aurlandsfjord, Todd Saunders & Tommie Wilhelmsen created the spectacular curving Stegastein lookout (2005), while Saunders also produced the refined CorTen steel and wood Solberg Tower and rest area (2010). Snøhetta's Eggum (2007), located in the Lofoten Islands, includes a concrete facilities building within an amphitheatre constructed of stone gabion walls.

Blueshuset (2014) which houses a variety of cultural institutions in Notodden.

Religious buildings continue to be important in Norway. Jensen & Skodvin's Mortensrud Church (2002) in Oslo is an elegant glass enclosure with the sanctuary nested within it and defined by a steel structure supporting an un-mortared stone triforium. Their Cistercian monastery Tautra Maria (2006), on the island of Tautra in the Trondheimfjord, is an expressive work with a slate exterior, glazed roof and a curved wooden lattice sanctuary. Terje Grønmo's white sculptured concrete Vardåsen Church (2003)

in Asker has an elegant light-filled sanctuary, while Askim Lantto Arkitekter's wood visitors' centre (2005) for the Borgund Stave Church focuses on the historic building and cemetery. The elegant light-filled Bøler Church (2011) in Oslo, by Hansen/Bjørndal Arkitekter, is a refined modernist work executed in wood, brick and concrete.

Formed around a courtyard and referencing Sami culture, the wood and concrete Sami Parliament of Norway (2005) in Kárášjohka (Karasjok), by Stein Halvorsen and Christian Sundby, features a peaked Sami tipi form for the plenary assembly hall.

Reiulf Ramstad Architects completed the extensive Trollstigen visitor centre (2009) at Møre og Romsdal, an essay in concrete and CorTen steel (Fig. 7.16), the cantilevered steel and glass Gaularfjellet viewing platform (2009) at Sogn og Fjordane, the concrete undulating walkway and spaces of seaside Selvika (2012) near Havøysund and the elegantly sited spikey glass Troll Wall restaurant and visitors' centre (2011) near Trollstigen. At Atnasjön

is Carl-Viggo Hølmebakk's raised curved concrete Sohlbergplassen viewpoint (2005), while at Nedre Oscarshaug he executed the more conceptual glass telescope (1997) (see Fig. 1.2). At Mefjellet, artist Kurt Wold created a stone sculpture (1997) framing the Fanaråken glacier, while 70°N arkitektur created a wood and glass building for cyclists (2005) at Grunnfør. A unique work is the gold-plated faceted restroom (2014) on the

beach at Ersfjordstranda by Tupelo Arkitekter.

Truly unique is a governmental agency that sponsors and realizes such a constellation of exemplary art, architectural and landscape architectural works, attesting to the significant cultural, architectural and environmental legacy initiated and nurtured by the Norwegian Public Roads Administration.

Fig 7.16 On the Norwegian National Tourist Route the expansive Trollstigen visitor centre (2009) at Møre og Romsdal, by Reiulf Ramstad Arkitekter, has a concrete and CorTen steel lookout point providing a dramatic view of the glacier-formed valley below. (Photo: Krysta Mae Dimick)

Foreign 'Starchitects' and Architects in the North

As Scandinavian architects have entered the global market and successfully competed for projects in North America, Asia, Africa, the Middle East and of course Europe, so too have international signature architects worked in the North. With today's information infrastructure and channels of interaction, both cross-pollination and collision of architectural ideas and expression are givens in current practice. Common throughout contemporary international practice is that 'starchitects', in addition to other well-known practitioners, often produce highly individualized work embracing a well-recognized personal aesthetic. These works can be, but are not always, created with little respect for locale or the challenges of the North. So are works by these architects influenced by the North? In some cases yes and in others no.

Recent examples of works produced by international architects and starchitects include a variety of projects and approaches but without question these are predominantly civic and cultural buildings often procured through competitions. The American Stephen Holl has executed the white concrete Herning Museum of Contemporary Art (2009) in Denmark which assumes the form of a collection of shirtsleeves with the interior spaces expressing textile qualities; while above the Arctic Circle is the Knut Hamsun Centre (2010) in Hamarøy, Norway – a roof garden tops a tower in black-stained wood which contrasts with its white interior. Spanish architect Santiago Calatrava's 54-storey Turning Torso (2005) in Malmö, the world's first twisting skyscraper and Scandinavia's tallest building, is an iconic Calatrava work. Zaha Hadid, an Iraqi-British architect, executed the Ordrupgaard Museum annexe (2005) in Denmark, which is constructed in glass and black lava concrete joined together to create an idiosyncratic flowing organic addition. In Ørestad, the blue exterior projection-screened Copenhagen Concert Hall (2009) by French architect Jean Nouvel awaits evening time

to achieve its full illuminated expression. Viennese firm Coop Himmelb(l)au's House of Music (2014) in Aalborg is an elemental deconstructivist essay in metal, concrete and glass. Italian architect Renzo Piano's wood and steel Astrup Fearnley Museum of Modern Art (2012), with its dynamic swooping glass roof, is located on the Oslo waterfront. The British firm Foster & Partners created the organic wave form of the Falun red Västra Årstabron (2005), or western Årsta Bridge.

London-based Brisac Gonzalez Architects executed the concrete and glass Museum of World Culture (2004) in Gothenburg, while the elemental white concrete and glass library and concert hall (2014) in the harbour of Bodø, Norway, is by the London studio of DRDH Architects. The faceted surfaced metal panel and glass School of Education and Library (2005) in Malmö is by the Swiss firm Diener & Diener. An evocative small corrugated metal free-form sculptural bathing pavilion (2014) in Gothenburg harbour is by raumlabor, a Berlin firm.

More is coming: the new Munch/Stenersen Museum near the Oslo Opera House is being designed by the Spanish firm Abalos & Herreros; the new Nobel Centre in Stockholm, Sweden, is in planning by David Chipperfield Architects of Berlin; and the Guggenheim Helsinki was awarded to the Japanese firm of Moreau Kusunoki Architectes. There is little question that the cross-fertilization and intellectual interchange occurring globally will continue to engage Nordic architecture and architects.

Modernism: The Continuing Thread through the Global Cacophony

For the past century plus, Nordic architecture has been acknowledged for its clarity of design and content, its strong adaptation to the surroundings and for being well grounded socially and functionally. In the late 1980s Juhani Pallasmaa stated that 'Modernism is the self-evident architectural condition of the Nordic democracies …' and continued, 'The mission of Nordic architecture lies in the continuous development of the tradition of socially concerned, responsive and assimilative Modernism.'[44]

But the face of architecture is transforming due to globalization's impact on economies and electronic communications and social interactions. The West held the hegemony on modern architecture during the twentieth century, with the participation of Latin America and Japan. Today the new large economies – China, India and Brazil – with the Second and Third World countries and regions are changing the dynamics and directions of architectural development. One need only follow the online list services on architecture to witness this evolution and the extensive number of new projects being proposed, developed and built globally. The webpages of current Nordic practitioners include the numerous international projects they are planning or have completed and the competitions they have entered. Many are in the emerging economies and countries, especially the Middle East, China, South-East Asia and Africa.

Within the 'starchitects' phenomenon is the potential of global homogenization or standardization of consumer products, including architecture. As architecture becomes commodified the devaluation of cultural differences occurs – differences necessary to codify our identity and existence. In danger of becoming lost is architecture based on the unique local conditions and traditions of a particular place; architecture rooted to a specific landscape, climate,

culture and history. While some Nordic architecture of this century appears formalistic in its expression, a majority of the work continues to exhibit its rootedness in the Northern world and to its conditions. So far it has been an imaginative time, where the global and local productively play off each other with stimulating results.

The Nordic desire to create modern, progressive, industrialized, urban and democratic societies that began a century and a quarter ago has matured to fruition. Today, the Scandinavian countries are globally acknowledged to be among the best places to live in the world by most metrics. Contributing to this well-being is the long-standing investment Scandinavian countries have made in their physical environment; in their architecture. There is little question that a majority of the Scandinavian architecture produced in this century continues the creative threads of modernism while providing the human face of the welfare state. The innovative civic and public works produced for cultural and governmental institutions; the responsive buildings created for education, health-care and elder- and childcare; the exciting new housing paradigms and forms of expression; and urban interventions that could only occur in cities where water, rock formations and forests require response, all attest to this. After more than a century, modernism continues to mature, adapt, assimilate and serve the Nordic world and its people: Nordic modernism continues to be alive.

1. Alvar Aalto, 'Eliel Saarinen' (eulogy delivered at Eliel Saarinen's state funeral in 1950), quoted in Göran Schildt (ed.), *Alvar Aalto: In His Own Words* (New York, 1998), p.244.

2. The Nordic countries are a geographical and cultural region, commonly known as 'Norden' – the North Land. It consists of five countries: Denmark, Sweden, Finland, Norway and Iceland and their autonomous regions (the Åland Islands, the Faroe Islands and Greenland). Politically, Nordic countries do not form a separate entity, but they cooperate in the Nordic Council. 'Scandinavia' is sometimes used as a synonym for the Nordic countries, but the term refers to the three monarchies of Denmark, Norway and Sweden.

3. Edward T. Hall and Mildred Reed Hall, *The Fourth Dimension in Architecture: The Impact of Building on Behaviour* (Santa Fe, NM: Sunstone, 1975), pp.8–9.

4. Robert Pogue Harrison, *Gardens: An Essay on the Human Condition* (Chicago: University of Chicago Press, 2008), p.130.

5. Maurice Merleau-Ponty, quoted in Iain McGilchrist, *The Master and His Emissary: The Divided Brain and the Making of the Western World* (New Haven, CT: Yale University Press, 2009), p.409.

6. 'Vakrare vardagsvara' ('More Beautiful Everyday Objects') was a 1919 essay by Gregor Paulsson for an exhibition in Gothenburg. The ideal was inspired by the German *Werkbund* and the notion became a slogan for the Swedish Craft Society. Later it was widely used in Nordic design and craft circles.

7. Göran Schildt, *Alvar Aalto: The Early Years* (New York: Rizzoli, 1984), p.207.

8. Alvar Aalto, 'The Decline of Public Buildings', *Arkkitehti*, No. 9–20, quoted in Schildt, *In His Own Words*, p.211.

9. Christian Norberg-Schulz, *Nightlands: Nordic Building* (Cambridge, MA: MIT Press, 1996), p.2.

10. Alvar Aalto, interview for Finnish television, July 1972, quoted in Schildt, *In His Own Words*, p.274.

11. Christian Norberg-Schulz, *Genius Loci: Towards a Phenomenology of Architecture* (New York: Rizzoli, 1980), p.42.

12. Norberg-Schulz, *Nightlands*, p.6.

13. Vesa Ibler, 'The Birth Gift of the 60th Latitude', in Marianne Ibler (ed.), *A New Golden Age – Nordic Architecture and Design* (Copenhagen: Archipress M, 2014), p.16.

14. Reima Pietilä, quoted in Henry Plummer, *Nordic Light: Modern Scandinavian Architecture* (New York: Thames & Hudson, 2012), p.120.

15. Paul Spreiregen, *Design Competitions* (New York: McGraw-Hill, 1979), p.79.

16. Hans Jacob Sparre, 'Norsk arkitektur, dens nuværend standpunkt og dens fremtidsudsigter' ('Norwegian Architecture, Its Present Position and Future Prospects'), lecture in Kristiania, 1901, published in *Teknisk Ugeblad*, 45 (1902). Quoted in Mari Hvattum, 'Making Place', *New Nordic Architecture and Identity* (Humlebæk, Denmark: Louisiana Museum of Modern Art, 2012), p.107.

17. Quoted in Nils Erik Wickberg, *Finnish Architecture* (Helsinki: Otava, 1962), p.85.

18. *Ibid.*, p.85.

19. Alvar Aalto, 'Architecture in the Landscape of Central Finland', *Sisä-Suomi*, 26 June 1925, quoted in Schildt, *In His Own Words*, p.22.

20. *Ibid.*, p.22.

21. *Ibid.*, p.22.

22. For additional information, see *Profiles: Pioneering Women Architects in Finland* (Helsinki: Museum of Finnish Architecture, 1983), 72 pp.

23. Mogens Lassen quoted in Nils-Ole Lund, 'Funktionalismen I Danmark' ('Functionalism in Denmark'), in Gunilla Lundahl (ed.), *Nordisk Funktionalism* (*Nordic Functionalism*) (Stockholm: Arkitektur Forlag, 1980), p.55.

24. Lars Backer, 'Our Spineless Architecture', *Byggekunst* (1925), quoted in Christian Norberg-Schulz, *Modern Norwegian Architecture* (Oslo: Norwegian University Press, 1986), p.47.

25. Hilding Ekelund writing in a review of an exhibition on rationalizing housing published in *Hufvudstadbladet* in the autumn of 1930, quoted in Kirmo Mikkola, 'På spaning efter en nutid' ('Looking for the Present Time'), in Lundahl (ed.), *Nordisk Funktionalism*, p.75.

26. See Le Corbusier, *The Radiant City* (New York: Orion, 1967); first published in 1933, this work fully outlines his ideas on city planning.

27. Esbjorn Hiort, *Nyere Dansk Bygningsunst/Contemporary Danish Architecture* (Copenhagen: Jul. Gjellerups Forlag, 1949), p.47.

28. *Ibid.*, p.24.

29. Alvar Aalto, 'Rationalismen och Manniskan' ('Rationalism and Man'), lecture delivered to the Swedish Craft Society, 9 May 1935, quoted in Göran Schildt (ed.), *Alvar Aalto: Sketches* (Cambridge, MA: MIT Press, 1978), p.48.

30. Alvar Aalto, 'The Humanizing of Architecture', *The Technology Review* (November 1940), pp.14–16.

31. Erik Gunnar Asplund, 'Konst och Teknik' ('Art and Technology'), speech presented to the Swedish Architectural Association, 1936, quoted in Stuart Wrede, *The Architecture of Erik Gunnar Asplund* (Cambridge, MA: MIT Press, 1980), p.153.

32. Asplund's Woodland Crematorium complex is one of two most written-about Nordic buildings in the past half-century. Alvar and Aino Aalto's Villa Mairea is the other. There is an extensive architectural literature on both works.

33. For a more extensive discussion of the relationship between the Aaltos' architecture and applied designs, see two essays by William C. Miller: 'Furniture, Painting and Applied Designs: Alvar Aalto's Search for Architectural Form', *Journal of Decorative and Propaganda Arts* (Fall 1987), pp.6–25; and 'Furniture, Painting and Applied Design: Small Rehearsals in Alvar Aalto's Search for Architectural Form', *ptah* (Journal of the Alvar Aalto Academy, Finland), No. 2 (2006), pp.36–48.

34. William C. Miller, 'A Thematic Analysis of Alvar Aalto's Architecture', *Architecture and Urbanism* (Japan), No. 109 (October 1979), pp.15–38.

35. Alvar and Aino Aalto's Villa Mairea is one of two most written-about Nordic buildings in the past half-century. Asplund's Woodland Crematorium complex is the other. There is an extensive architectural literature on both works.

36. 'Quotations from Kay Fisker: Svensk Bygningskunst', *Arkitekten. Ugehæfte* (1945), pp.30–32, quoted in Nils-Ole Lund, *Nordic Architecture* (Copenhagen: Arkitektens Forlag/Danish Architectural Press, 2008), p.162.

37. Françoise Fromonot, *Jørn Utzon: The Sydney Opera House* (Milan: Electa, 2000), 236 pp.

38. For a detailed account of postmodernism, see Charles Jencks, *The Language of Post-Modern Architecture* (New York: Rizzoli, 1977), 104 pp. The work is now in its sixth edition (1991, 204 pp).

39. For a discussion of deconstructivism, see Phillip Johnson and Mark Wigley, *Deconstructivist Architecture: The Museum of Modern Art* (New York: Little, Brown, 1988), 104 pp.

40. Kenneth Frampton, 'Towards a Critical Regionalism: Six Points for an Architecture of Resistance', in Hal Foster (ed.), *The Anti-Aesthetic: Essays on Postmodern Culture* (Port Townsend, WA: Bay Press, 1983), pp.16–30.

41. The best assessment of Erik Asmussen's work and the Järna complex is Gary J. Coates, *Erik Asmussen, Architect* (Stockholm: Byggförlaget, 1997), 240 pp.

42. Juhani Pallasmaa, *The Eyes of the Skin: Architecture and the Senses* (London: Academy Editions, 1996), p.28.

43. The Pritzker Prize honours a living architect or architects whose built work demonstrates a combination of talent, vision and commitment which has produced consistent and significant contributions through the art of architecture. It is an international prize granted annually and is often referred to as 'architecture's Nobel' and 'the profession's highest honour'. To date two Nordic architects have received the prize: Sverre Fehn and Jørn Utzon. For additional information go to www.pritzkerprize.com.

44. Juhani Pallasmaa, 'Tradition and Modernity: The Feasibility of Regional Architecture in Post-Modern Society', lecture delivered at the 'Nordic Tradition' conference in Copenhagen, 1988, reprinted in *Encounters: Architectural Essays*, ed. Peter MacKeith (Helsinki: Rakennustieto, 2005), pp.277–278.

Bibliography

Aalto, Alvar, 'The Humanizing of Architecture', *The Technology Review* (November 1940, pp.14–16)

Ahlin, Jaanne, *Sigurd Lewerentz, Architect 1885–1975* (Cambridge, MA: MIT Press, 1987)

Asensio, Paco (ed.), *New Scandinavian Design* (New York: teNeues, 2005)

Bengtsson, Staffan and Sandra Nolgren, *Norway Calling: Touch-Down in a World of Norwegian Design* (Stockholm: Arvinius Förlag, 2008)

Berglund, Kristina and Hisashi Tanaka (eds), *Swedish Contemporary Architecture*, Process: Architecture series, No. 68 (Tokyo: Process Architecture, 1986)

Berman, Patricia G. (ed.), *Luminous Modernism: Scandinavian Art Comes to America – A Centennial Retrospective 1912–2012* (New York: American-Scandinavian Foundation, 2011)

Berman, Patricia G. and Thor J. Mednick (eds), *Danish Paintings from the Golden Age to the Modern Breakthrough: Selections from the Collection of Ambassador John L. Loeb Jr.* (New York: American-Scandinavian Foundation, 2013)

BIG/Bjarke Ingels Group: Recent Project (Tokyo: A.D.A. Edita, 2012)

Bugge, Gunnar, *Stave Churches in Norway* (Oslo: Dreyers Forlag, 1983)

Caldenby, Claes and Olof Hultin, *Asplund* (New York: Rizzoli, 1986)

Caldenby, Claes, Jöran Lindvall, Wilfred Wand and Thorbjorn Andersson, *Twentieth Century Architecture: Sweden* (Munich: Prestel, 1998)

Chang, Ching-Yu (ed.), *A Perspective of Modern Scandinavian Architecture* Process: Architecture series, No. 1 (Tokyo and Forest Grove, OR: Process Architecture, 1977)

Coates, Gary J., *Erik Asmussen, Architect* (Stockholm: Byggförlaget, 1997)

Constant, Caroline, *The Woodland Cemetery: Toward a Spiritual Landscape* (Stockholm: Byggförlaget, 1994)

Davey, Peter, *Heikkinen & Komonen*, ed. Xavier Güell (Barcelona: Gustavo Gili, 1994)

Donnelly, Marian C., *Architecture in the Scandinavian Countries* (Cambridge, MA: MIT Press, 1992)

Edam, Carl Tomas, Nils-Göran Hökby and Birgitta Schreiber, *Scandinavian Modernism: Painting in Denmark, Finland, Iceland, Norway and Sweden 1910–1920* (New York: Rizzoli, 1989)

Egelius, Mats, *Ralph Erskine, Architect* (Stockholm: Byggförlaget, 1990)

Faber, Tobias, *A History of Danish Architecture* (Copenhagen: Det Danske Selskab, 1978)

Fjeld, Per Olaf, *Sverre Fehn: The Thought of Construction* (New York: Rizzoli, 1983)

——, *Sverre Fehn: The Pattern of Thoughts* (New York: Monacelli, 2009)

Fleig, Karl (ed.), *Alvar Aalto: Volume I 1922–62* (Zurich: Artemis, 1963)

——, *Alvar Aalto: Volume II, 1963–70* (Zurich: Artemis, 1971)

——, *Alvar Aalto: Volume III, Projects and Final Buildings* (Zurich: Artemis, 1978)

Flore, Nicola, Paolo Giardiello and Gennaro Postiglione, *Sigurd Lewerentz 1885–1975* (Milan: Electa Architecture, 2002)

Foster, Hal (ed.), *The Anti-Aesthetic: Essays on Postmodern Culture* (Port Townsend, WA: Bay Press, 1983)

Fromonot, Françoise, *Jørn Utzon: The Sydney Opera House* (Milan: Electra, 2000)

Gullichsen, Kirsi and Ulla Kinnunen, *Inside the Villa Mairea: Art, Design and Interior Architecture* (Helsinki: Alvar Aalto Museum and Mairea Foundation, 2009)

Gunnarsson, Torsten, *Nordic Landscape Painting in the Nineteenth Century* (New Haven, CT: Yale University Press, 1998)

Hall, Edward T. and Mildred Reed Hall, *The Fourth Dimension in Architecture: The Impact of Building on Behaviour* (Santa Fe, NM: Sunstone, 1975)

Harrison, Robert Pogue, *Gardens: An Essay on the Human Condition* (Chicago: University of Chicago Press, 2008)

Hiort, Esbjorn, *Nyere Dansk Bygningsunst/Contemporary Danish Architecture* (Copenhagen: Jul. Gjellerups Forlag, 1949)

Hipeli, Mia and Esa Laaksonen (eds), *Alvar Aalto Architect: Paimio Sanatorium 1929–33* (Helsinki: Alvar Aalto Foundation and Rakennustieto, 2014)

Hvattum, Mari, 'Making Place', *New Nordic Architecture and Identity* (Humlebæk, DK: Louisiana Museum of Modern Art, 2012)

Ibler, Marianne, *A New Golden Age – Nordic Architecture and Design* (Copenhagen: Archipress M, 2014)

Ingels, Bjarke (ed.), *Yes is More: An Archicomic on Architectural Evolution* (Copenhagen: Evergreen, 2009)

Jencks, Charles, *The Language of Post-Modern Architecture* (New York: Rizzoli, 1977; 6th edition 1991)

Johnson, Phillip and Mark Wigley, *Deconstructivist Architecture: The Museum of Modern Art* (New York: Little, Brown, 1988)

Jones, Peter Blundell, *Gunnar Asplund* (London: Phaidon, 2006)

Kent, Neil, *The Triumph of Light and Nature: Nordic Art 1740–1940* (London: Thames & Hudson, 1987)

—, *The Soul of the North: A Social, Architectural and Cultural History of the Nordic Countries, 1700–1940* (London: Reaktion, 2000)

Kidder Smith, G.E., *Sweden Builds* (New York: Reinhold, 1957).

Kjeldsen, K., J.R. Schelde, M.A. Andersen and M.J. Holm (eds), *New Nordic Architecture and Identity* (Humlebæk, Denmark: Louisiana Museum of Modern Art, 2012)

Korvenmaa, Pekka (ed.), *The Work of Architects: The Finnish Association of Architects 1892–1992* (Helsinki: Finnish Building Centre, 1992)

Lahti, Markku and Maija Holma, *Alvar Aalto: A Gentler Structure for Life* (Helsinki: Rakennustieto, 1996)

Lane, Barbara Miller, *National Romanticism and Modern Architecture in Germany and the Scandinavian Countries* (Cambridge, UK: Cambridge University Press, 2000)

Le Corbusier, *The Radiant City* (New York: Orion, 1967)

Lund, Nils-Ole, *Nordic Architecture* (Copenhagen: Arkitektens Forlag/Danish Architecture Press, 2008).

Lundahl, Gunilla (ed.), *Nordisk Funktionalism* (*Nordic Functionalism*) (Stockholm: Arkitektur Forlag, 1980)

McGilchrist, Iain, *The Master and His Emissary: The Divided Brain and the Making of the Western World* (New Haven, CT: Yale University Press, 2009)

Miller, William C., 'A Thematic Analysis of Alvar Aalto's Architecture', *Architecture and Urbanism* (Japan), No. 109 (October 1979, pp.15–38)

—, 'Furniture, Painting and Applied Designs: Alvar Aalto's Search for Architectural Form', *Journal of Decorative and Propaganda Arts* (Fall 1987, pp.6–25)

—, 'Scandinavian Architecture during the Late 1930s: Asplund and Aalto vs. Functionalism', *Reflections* (Journal of the School of Architecture, University of Illinois at Urbana-Champaign), No. 7 (1990, pp.4–13)

—, 'Furniture, Painting and Applied Design: Small Rehearsals in Alvar Aalto's Search for Architectural Form', *ptah* (Journal of the Alvar Aalto Academy, Finland), No. 2 (2006, pp.36–48)

Nikula, Riitta (ed.), *Erik Bryggman 1891–1955* (Helsinki: Museum of Finnish Architecture, 1991)

Norberg-Schulz, Christian, *Genius Loci: Towards a Phenomenology of Architecture* (New York: Rizzoli, 1980)

—, *Modern Norwegian Architecture* (Oslo: Universitetsforlaget, 1986)

—, *The Functionalist Arne Korsmo* (Oslo: Universitetsforlaget, 1986)

—, *Nightlands: Nordic Building* (Cambridge, MA: MIT Press, 1996)

Norberg-Schulz, Christian and Gennaro Postiglione, *Sverre Fehn: Works, Projects, Writings 1949–1996* (New York: Monacelli. 1997)

Nordic Models + Common Ground: Art and Design Unfolded (New York: American-Scandinavian Foundation, 2010)

Norri, Marja-Riitta and Kristiina Paatero (eds), *Juha Leiviskä* (Helsinki: Museum of Finnish Architecture, 1999)

Norri, Marja-Riitta, Elina Standertskjöld and Wilfred Wang (eds), *Twentieth Century Architecture: Finland* (Helsinki: Museum of Finnish Architecture, 2000)

Okkonen, Onni, *Finnish Art* (Helsinki: Werner Söderström OY, 1946)

Ostrowski, Stefan, Annika Wingårdh, Graham Timmins and Magnus Cimmerbeck, *Nordic by Nature: Modern Swedish Architecture Integrating Mind and Tradition in New Designs for Living and Working* (Stockholm: LTs Förlag, 2001) (This volume focuses on the architecture of Gert Wingårdh.)

Paavilainen, Simo (ed.), *Nordisk Klassicism 1910–1930/Nordic Classicism 1910–1930* (Helsinki: Museum of Finnish Architecture, 1982)

Pallasmaa, Juhani, *The Eyes of the Skin: Architecture and the Senses* (London: Academy Editions, 1996)

—, *Encounters: Architectural Essays*, edited by Peter MacKeith (Helsinki: Rakennustieto, 2005)

—, *Encounters 2: Architectural Essays*, edited by Peter MacKeith (Helsinki: Rakennustieto, 2012)

Pallasmaa, Juhani (ed.), *Villa Mairea 1938–39* (Helsinki: Alvar Aalto Foundation and Mairea Foundation, 1998)

Pearson, Paul David, *Alvar Aalto and the International Style* (New York: Whitney Library of Design, 1978)

Pietilä, Reima, *Pietilä: Intermediate Zones in Modern Architecture* (Helsinki, Museum of Finnish Architecture, 1978)

Plummer, Henry, *Nordic Light: Modern Scandinavian Architecture* (New York: Thames & Hudson, 2012)

Poole, Scott, *The New Finnish Architecture* (New York: Rizzoli, 1992)

Postiglione, Gennaro and Mareike Henschel (eds), *Nineteen Thirties Nordic Architecture* (Milan: Politecnico di Milano, 2002)

Profiles: Pioneering Women Architects in Finland (Helsinki: Museum of Finnish Architecture, 1983)

Quantrill, Malcolm, *Finnish Architecture and the Modernist Tradition* (London: E. & F.N. Spon, 1995)

Rudberg, Eva, *Sven Markelius, Arkitekt* (Stockholm: Arkitektur Förlag, 1989)

—, *The Stockholm Exhibition 1930: Modernism's Breakthrough in Swedish Architecture* (Stockholm: Arkitektur Förlag, 1999)

Schildt, Göran, *Alvar Aalto: The Early Years* (New York: Rizzoli, 1984)

Schildt, Göran (ed.), *Alvar Aalto: Sketches* (Cambridge, MA: MIT Press, 1978)

—, *Alvar Aalto: In His Own Words* (New York: Rizzoli, 1998)

Skriver, Poul Erik and Ellen Waade, *Arne Jacobsen* (Copenhagen: Danish Bicentennial Committee, 1976)

Snøhetta (ed.), *Snøhetta Works* (Baden, Germany: Lars Müller, 2009)

Sokol, David, *Nordic Architects* (Stockholm: Arvinius Förlag, 2008)

—, *Nordic Architects: Ebbs and Flows* (Stockholm: Arvinius + Orfeus, 2013)

Solaguren-Beascoa, Félix (ed.), 'Arne Jacobsen: Edificios Públicos/Public Buildings', *Revista Internacional de Arquitectura*, No. 4 (1997), 144 pp.

Spreiregen, Paul, *Design Competitions* (New York: McGraw-Hill, 1979)

Stewart, John, *Nordic Classical Architecture* (Stockholm: Arvinius + Orfeus, 2016)

Thau, Carsten and Kjeld Vindum, *Arne Jacobsen* (Copenhagen: Arkitektens Forlag, 2001)

Thiis-Evensen, Thomas, *The Postmodernists Jan and Jon* (Oslo: Universitetsforlaget, 1984)

Tschudi-Madsen, Stephen, *Henrik Bull* (Oslo: Universitetsforlaget, 1983)

Varnedoe Kirk, *Northern Light: Nordic Art at the Turn of the Century* (New Haven, CT: Yale University Press, 1988)

Weston, Richard, *Villa Mairea* (London: Phaidon, 1992)

—, *Alvar Aalto* (London: Phaidon, 1998)

—, *Utzon: Inspiration, Vision, Architecture* (Copenhagen: Edition Bløndal, 2002)

Wickberg, Nils Erik, *Finnish Architecture* (Helsinki: Otava, 1962)

Wilson, Colin St John, *Gullichsen/Kairamo/Vormala*, ed. Xavier Güell (Barcelona: Gustavo Gili, 1990)

Wrede, Stuart, *The Architecture of Erik Gunnar Asplund* (Cambridge, MA: MIT Press, 1980)

Yoshizaki, Keiko (ed.), *Finnish Architecture Now*, Process: Architecture series, No. 37 (Tokyo: Process Architecture, 1983)

An entry in **bold** indicates an illustration or photograph.